GOLF

ETIQUETTE

GOLF
ETIQUETTE

BARBARA PUETT AND JIM APFELBAUM

ILLUSTRATIONS BY CARRELL GRIGSBY

ST. MARTIN'S PRESS
NEW YORK

GOLF ETIQUETTE. Copyright © 1992 by Barbara Puett and Jim Apfelbaum. All rights reserved. Printed in the United States of America. No part of this book may be reproduced in any manner whatsoever without written permission except in the case of brief quotations embodied in critical articles or reviews. For information, address St. Martin's Press, 175 Fifth Avenue, New York, N.Y. 10010.

Design by Robert Bull Design

Library of Congress Cataloging-in-Publication Data

Puett, Barbara.
   Golf etiquette / Barbara Puett and Jim Apfelbaum; foreword by Tom Kite
     p.   cm.
   ISBN 0-312-07686-X
   1. Golf. 2 Etiquette.   I. Apfelbaum, Jim.   II. Title.
  GV965.P84   1992
796.352—dc20   92-4102
                                                       CIP

First Edition: July 1992

10 9 8 7 6 5 4 3

CONTENTS

NOTE TO THE READER: Each chapter is followed by a glossary. Several definitions deliberately appear in the glossary but not in the chapter. In a sport that continues to generate more slang than the average teenager, it would be impossible to keep pace. We have endeavored to include those terms and phrases unfamiliar to newer golfers, all too often omitted from standard glossaries, that are still commonly heard on the golf course.

FOREWORD
BY TOM KITE

Most of us who consider ourselves golfers have at one time or another been confounded and confused by the Rules of Golf. Some even consider the Rule Book to be too lengthy or not appropriate for today's game or just too much of a bother. After all, they say, the game is difficult enough without having to play by the strictest of rules.

But one part of the rules that should not be ignored by anyone who wishes to have someone else to play with is the Rules of Etiquette. Obviously the USGA, the rule-making body, feels that proper golf etiquette is important. That is why they chose to put some suggestions at the front of every Rule Book.

And as the game continues to grow in popularity, the Rules of Etiquette become even more important. They are what separate golf from other sports and allow all players of different handicap levels to have a good time, even on the days the putts don't drop.

This book is long overdue. If this were a college course, it would be must reading. And whether or not you have the inclination and courage to wade through the Rules of Golf, reading and abiding by *Golf Etiquette* will help ensure that you and your playing partners will always enjoy golf.

TOM KITE

PREFACE

This is not an instruction book. It won't help you hit it farther or even cure your slice. But no matter how you play, this book will help you enjoy golf more fully. With an understanding of the accepted courtesies of the course, golfers can play comfortably with one another anywhere in the world.

Etiquette pervades all levels of golf, which prides itself on sportsmanship. "The sum total of the rules [of etiquette]," wrote Abe Mitchell, a British champion, "is thoughtfulness." Thoughtfulness applies equally to beginners as it does to experts. With little effort, it can (and should) be practiced by everyone who plays golf: man, woman, or child. In the authors' opinion, slow play, golf's biggest problem, could be alleviated, if not erradicated altogether, if every golfer observed the common-sense rules of decorum that have served the game so well.

The problem with golf etiquette, as with etiquette in other social circumstances, is that mistakes cannot be disguised. You either know it or you don't, whether it involves a salad fork or a putting line. By the time you step out on the course, if you don't already know the Rules of Etiquette, it's too late. When golf wasn't so popular, transgressions were easier to overlook.

That's a luxury the game can no longer afford. Golf once strolled along two-lane roads; today it clogs superhighways.

We've tried to demystify the Rules of Etiquette that new golfers especially find so bewildering. Fortunately, the right ways are no harder to master than the wrong ways.

Harvey Penick, a past PGA Teacher of the Year and source of much of the common sense described within, has said: "I can't think of anything that would lend itself more to the enjoyment of the game than knowing the Rules of Etiquette." If his name doesn't ring a bell, perhaps you've heard of two of his students, Tom Kite and Ben Crenshaw. Both have achieved tremendous success by any measure one chooses. Beyond mere tournament wins or prize money, however, both have been honored as recipients of the Bob Jones Award for distinguished sportsmanship in golf, the highest honor given by the United States Golf Association. We'd like to take this opportunity to also thank them both for their contributions.

BEFORE YOU PLAY

FROM SILK TO SANSABELT

GOLF IS A gentleman's game. Good sportsmanship and fair play still count for something. Since golf remains, for 99.9 percent of us, at least as much social as sporting, it's no wonder dressing a good game still counts for something, too.

Unlike other athletes, golfers wear no official uniform. (The Professional Golfers Association PGA Tour—once experimented with numbers on the backs of competitors, but the players refused to go along.) Without specific guidelines, questions of appropriate dress are largely left to individual discretion and judgment, as so much in golf is.

Scores are not affected for violations of the game's stylish legacy. The toll exacted is far more penal—an unmistakably frosty reception, perhaps an icy stare, or worse, no second invitation to play. One thing is certain: when these traditions are ignored or flouted, the game and the golfer both lose a little something.

No one set a more enduring sartorial standard than Walter Hagen. The flamboyant champion of the 1920s bought his *plus fours* on Savile Row, his shirts from Sulka, and his ties from Hermés. His elegance would stand out today—on or off the golf course.

Another popular professional, Jimmy Demaret, later unlocked a postwar Pandora's box of vibrant colors and styles.

Pink, aqua, and emerald came out of the crayon box. Shades more suited to the breakfast table followed: lemon-lime, cantaloupe, grape, banana. The closets of otherwise conventional businessmen would never be the same.

Whether you prefer Egyptian cotton or Ban-Lon, silk or Sansabelt, Hagen or Demaret, there are no limits in extravagance or expense when it comes to golf attire, only degrees of appropriateness for a given situation.

Many courses observe a dress code that requires compliance to play, but as we've seen, there is plenty of room for personal expression. Dressing appropriately for golf is no different from dressing appropriately for any social occasion. On a ranch, jeans would certainly be appropriate; at a formal wedding, they would look ridiculous.

Modern golf fashion emphasizes comfort and function. Even if you hit every green and fairway *in regulation*, you will still be at the mercy of Mother Nature. You might find it expedient to stow a sweater, a windbreaker, or an extra pair of socks in your golf bag.

A GOOD RULE OF THUMB

There are no hard-and-fast rules about dress codes in golf. They vary from region to region and from course to course, even among courses of the same type. At country clubs, for example, what works at one may not work at another. Take nothing for granted. An advance call to the pro shop will discreetly dispel any doubts and avoid potential embarrassment.

Generally, as green fees rise, so do the dress requirements. On *municipal* or *public courses*, there may be a shortage of shirts. Neon surfing baggies, suspenders, you name it, they've been worn on a golf course. But just because they aren't printed on the scorecard doesn't mean the only bounds of decorum in play are the ones listed in local statutes under public decency.

Consider Pebble Beach. Perched over the Pacific, it is widely hailed as one of golf's true pearls. It's also as public as a parking space. Anyone willing to part with $225, and most likely several balls, can play. While black tie is not required, please don't expect to get on in jeans and a T-shirt. Why not? For the same reason that you don't wear blue jeans to formal weddings. It's just not done.

On *private daily fee courses*, collars on shirts (i.e., no T-shirts) are usually required. Whether an alligator, shark, umbrella, sombrero, etc., adorns the left breast is up to you. Blue jeans, cutoffs, or gym shorts may be prohibited. The restrictions are entirely arbitrary. It is your responsibility to learn and observe them.

Country clubs also vary their dress requirements. Although there are no hard-and-fast rules, the less expensive and less exclusive a club is, the more liberal its dress code; the fancier the club, the more formal the dress. (Club dress requirements off the course are discussed later in this chapter.)

WATCH YOUR STEP

Cowboy boots, high heels, or waffle-edged running shoes could easily make hash out of a green and are naturally barred. Golf shoes aren't always required, however. At the very least, tennis shoes or soft rubber-soled shoes are acceptable. Having said that, private clubs may specifically require cleated golf shoes to play the course. Once again, it's not cut-and-dried. It's your responsibility to find out beforehand. If you have any doubts about your attire, from shoes on up, call the pro shop.

To be on the safe side, boys or men should wear slacks, collared sport shirts, and a pair of golf shoes.

Note: While many (but not all) courses allow men to play in shorts, tennis or running shorts are not acceptable. A longer length short, identified by various names, is recommended. Again, it is wise to check beforehand. Ask specifically for the length of short permitted.

For men: Appropriate everywhere.

"WHEN THE PLAYER IS CLAD IN FEMALE DRESS"

We know that Mary, Queen of Scots, was playing golf a few days after the murder of her husband, Lord Darnley, in 1567. While Scottish women and children must surely have played in the interim, there are scant records of them doing so until the reign of Queen Victoria. If ever evidence were needed to prove the depth of golf's addictive properties, look no further than the Victorian woman golfer. She braved considerable hardships, not the least of which were her clothes.

In the 1870s, for example, long, full skirts, high-necked blouses, leg-of-mutton sleeves, a hat, and a bustle were the height of sporting fashion. Add the typical underwear for the well-dressed Victorian woman: camisole, chemise, corset, half a dozen petticoats, stockings, and garters, and walking the course—let alone finding the ball and hitting it—must've been a minor miracle. Ingenuity played its part. To combat typically blustery conditions, an elastic band was devised to be worn around the waist. Easily dropped down to the knees, it served to keep a billowing dress momentarily quiet during the swing.

There were more familiar hardships. In those days before women had ankles, one Lord Wellwood (you can almost see him in pipe and smoking jacket) blithely suggested that women contain their swings because "the posture and gesture required for a full swing are not particularly graceful when the player is clad in female dress." He may have received a hearty "here, here" from the boys at the club, but his idea of "women's rights" went unheeded.

There is a story that Joyce Wethered, one of the finest players of either sex in the 1920s, actually found a way to use her attire to advantage. She had her tweed skirts tailored to the precise width of her stance. When they pulled snugly at the knees during *address*, she knew her stance was correct.

Flexibility in fashion of a kind unknown in the past has become the norm. Golfers of both sexes, but especially women, are wearing clothes that work as well on the course as off. The classics remain: golf skirts or slacks, knee-length shorts, sport shirts. A more assimilated look, away from the more rigid ensembles of the past, offers additional choices: conservative, eclectic, trendy, traditional. One evidence of the change is the accepted variety in skirt lengths. Hemlines can be anywhere from thigh high to mid calf. Whether tartan or neon happens to be in vogue, the key word is, and always will be: comfort.

Mrs. Charles Brown, the first Women's U.S. Open Champion, 1895, clad in female dress. (COURTESY USGA)

On public courses, sweats, old sneakers, tank tops, or running shorts will suffice. On private daily fee courses or at country clubs, conventional wisdom calls for traditional golf shirts with collars, knee-length shorts, skirts or slacks. (Beware: jeans may also be prohibited or at least frowned upon.)

Women should be especially vigilant about dress codes. Pro shops are accustomed to dealing with people familiar with the requirements and often make general assumptions about "appropriate golf wear." Be specific with your questions. You may have to prod a little to find out that appropriate golf wear in fact means nothing less than shorts no higher than four inches above the knee, collared golf shirts, and cleated golf shoes.

THE LOGO LOOK

A century since it first became popular, the tam-o'-shanter still adorns shelves in well-stocked pro shops from Carnoustie to Carmel. Favored by the Scottish professionals who brought golf to England, admiring students adopted the tam (and perhaps even a little brogue) in the hope that it might improve their golf.

Such optimism continues unabated. Many golfers today sport the same corporate names or logos on their clothing as the professionals. This mimicry distresses some traditionalists. They lament commercialism's encroachment upon the epitome of professionalism and good taste that golf symbolizes. For them, *touring pros* bedecked in endorsements more closely resemble race cars or billboards.

There is nothing wrong with wearing logos, even if you are not paid to wear them. Frankly, it is almost impossible to avoid them on any sports apparel. You will have to be the judge. To make a good impression, a modest approach is best. For most of us, understatement is much easier to live with. Unfortunately, a champion's mien is no more within our grasp today by wearing his or her line of clothes than it was when the tam-o'-shanter first topped the fashion charts.

For women: Two styles, appropriate everywhere.

FRY NOW, PAY LATER

There is one cue you should take from the professionals, which-ever way the fashion winds blow. The American Cancer Society reports more than 600,000 new cases of skin cancer each year. A wide-brimmed hat or visor, a bandanna on the neck, long-sleeved shirts, long pants, and sunscreen are part of their recommendations. Hats have the added benefit of style, the signature of many golfing greats through the years.

A GOOD SWING CAN HIT ANY CLUB

Golf equipment continues to evolve and improve. Clubs are easier to hit than ever before. Balls fly farther and straighter. Still, science hacks away at golf. And still the slice and the missed three-foot putt remain, impervious as the common cold.

The explanation is simple: golf is not an exact science. Over the years, golf equipment has changed considerably; golf not so much, humans not at all.

Harvey Penick, who has tutored many champions, always said that a good swing can hit any club. It was his way of saying: get your mind off the equipment and concentrate on swinging correctly. No advice could be more sound.

Underneath the sunscreen of every golfer lies an equipment junkie waiting to happen. We're easy marks and always have been. Think selecting equipment is confusing today? Consider Horace Hutchinson's observation in 1890:

> There are long cleeks and short cleeks, driving cleeks, lofting cleeks, and putting cleeks; there are heavy irons and light irons, driving irons, lofting irons, and sand irons. There are mashies and niblicks. In this multitude of golf clubs there is wisdom—somewhere—but it can scarcely be that all of them are necessary.

The temptation to buy a better game persists today, as a glance in any golfer's basement or garage will attest. It is also expensive and rarely produces overnight success. As the golfer once wrote to thank the manufacturer of his new driver: "It has added 50 yards to my slice."

Bobby Jones is considered to be the finest golfer who ever

played. He never enjoyed the benefits of modern club technology: *cavity-backed designs*, *radiused soles*, or even *dual weightports*, whatever they are. Never mind. His achievements are no less remarkable. His perceptions remain as relevant today as they were when he competed more than a half-century ago. But it didn't start there. The same year Sir Isaac Newton defined the laws of gravity, a young medical student named Thomas Kincaid jotted down some thoughts on "playeing at golve" in his diary. His thoughts are consistent with the modern swing, and they were recorded in 1687!

No one denies that equipment has improved with time. The fact is, however, that numerous products today touted as new and revolutionary were patented as long ago as the turn of the century. These include such "modern" innovations as metal woods and deep-grooved irons, to name just two. The search for golf perfection is by no means new, and it will never end.

While we encourage every golfer to get the best equipment, expensive clubs are not a prerequisite to enjoying the game. Clubs may be new or used, from pro shop or garage sale. Used sets of better clubs are always a good buy.

Learn how to enjoy golf first. See if you even like the game. Then, if you get bitten, you'll feel more comfortable about making a greater financial commitment. The better you play, the more clubs make a difference. To begin, you need only a bag, some balls, and a few clubs (including a putter). A full set is not required. A serviceable mix (and one easy on the shoulders) might include the 3- , 5- , 7- , and 9-irons, a wedge and putter, a 5-wood, and a 3-wood for tee shots. The rules allow golfers to carry no more than fourteen clubs.

Clubs can be fitted to each golfer as much as any mass manufactured product can be. Height, hand size, and strength are some of the considerations. There's no question that fit is important, just as it is in getting the right-sized grip on a tennis racket or proper-length skis. Teaching professionals offer proper fitting and the benefit of their expertise for an almost infinite number of options. Try not to get too caught up in the hype of "new and improved." Remember, it's not what you swing but how you swing that's important. (A primer on some basic equipment terms is included in the glossary so you won't be completely in the dark.)

PETRIFIED CLUBS

Similar to cavity-backed designs on irons, metal woods provide a bigger sweet spot for those longer distance clubs traditionally made of wood: driver, 3-wood, 5-wood, etc. Metal woods are actually hollow inside or filled with foam. Although they are often recommended for beginners, golfers of all abilities swear by them. Now if only someone could come up with a better name for them.

GETTING THE SHAFT

Shafts are one of the most important considerations in club selection. The flexibility of the shaft should ideally match the strength and ability of the player. They can be either flexible, regular, or stiff. The point to remember is that in choosing clubs, you'll want to make sure you don't get the shaft, that is, one that is not right for you.

CAN I SEE THAT IN A 34 REGULAR?

Men's and women's clubs are not the same. Women's clubs are shorter, lighter, and usually have flexible shafts. Women taller than five feet six inches might consider lightweight men's clubs. Similarly, for a better fit, shorter men may want a shorter shaft. The number of available club options is perhaps rivaled only by the many ways of acquiring golf clubs. Wherever the search takes you, we strongly recommend getting some qualified help, especially if you're considering buying a new set.

Of course, price may be your biggest concern. Brand-new, top-of-the-line clubs are expensive. You might hunt the classified ads or the bulletin boards for a good set of used clubs that may need only a new set of grips to bring them up to snuff; or consider a set of fitted generic clubs that copy more expensive models.

A boon to travelers, club rentals are available at many courses. In an increasingly competitive business, golf club manufacturers have come up with enticing premiums and promotions. "Test drives" of new equipment are often offered at country clubs and driving ranges. Some sell single clubs through

The game may change but golfers have always craved distance.
A turn-of-the-century British ball advertisement. (Courtesy USGA)

the mail (usually a 7- or 5-iron) to whet your appetite to buy a full set. But let the buyer beware. Apply the same diligence and consumer savvy in buying golf clubs as in making any major purchase. It pays to shop around. Out on the course, it won't make any difference how much you paid for your clubs, only whether you can hit them.

THE R&A & THE USGA

The Royal and Ancient Golf Club of St. Andrews, Scotland, and the United States Golf Association (USGA) jointly govern the game of golf, administering the rules and guarding the game's traditions and integrity. Manufacturers searching for advantage sometimes go too far. The R&A and the USGA run exhaustive equipment tests to determine compliance. Some equipment has been deemed illegal. That doesn't mean that you can't use and enjoy it, only that it is not allowed in formal competition. Each golfer has to decide whether to observe the official recommendations.

FOLLOW THE BOUNCING OCTAHELIX DIMPLE PATTERN

Balls are on the front lines of the economic and ethical equipment battles. Some golfers fear that advances in equipment may render some of the game's most storied courses obsolete (although you won't hear them complaining about extra yards off the tee). All we can say is it hasn't happened yet. St. Andrews continues to entertain and challenge golfers as it has for centuries. After all, whether the ball is stuffed with feathers or liquid or rubber, golf remains a game of accuracy and consistency, not merely distance. Because balls fly farther doesn't mean they necessarily fly straighter.

Which ball you favor, like clubs, shafts, grips, or head covers, is a matter of personal preference. Golf has always been a fount of eccentricity and superstition. Some golfers won't play high-numbered balls because they think they encourage higher scores. Others prefer balls with the number 8 on them, in the belief that they offer better symmetry in flight. Who knows?

Shopping for golf balls can be confusing. On the outside of the box (commonly called a "sleeve"), you'll find various product descriptions. Like most products, golf balls are tailored to fit the needs of different clienteles. Three terms every golfer should have at least a working knowledge of are: *compression*, *balata*, and *surlyn*.

Compression is an industry yardstick that measures the hardness of the ball. The higher the compression the harder the ball. Three-piece balls have liquid centers wound with elastic and covered with balata rubber. They're said to be easier to put backspin on and curve more easily in flight, attributes that make them more appealing to professionals. Balata balls are, however, more susceptible to cuts and scuff marks.

Two-piece balls have a solid synthetic center covered with surlyn. They are believed to be the more durable of the two and roll farther, but are harder to put English on. Because of their

Golf bags come in many sizes and designs.

durability (not to mention the possibility of a few extra yards), two-piece surlyn balls at 90 compression are recommended.

We can make one unqualified endorsement. *X-out balls*, on most store and pro shop shelves, sell for considerably less than top-of-the-line models. Some golfers won't touch them, but for the average player they play as true as a regular ball in both velocity and distance. X-outs are factory overruns or balls with cosmetic blemishes. They're also brand-new (as opposed to the jar of used and possibly water-logged balls on pro shop counters). The ones with corporate logos or business names on them are the best of the bunch.

IN THE BAG

Golf bags come in astonishing varieties. Some strap on like backpacks; others come with pop-up legs. You'll find them in every color, from oxblood to fluorescent orange. Like luggage, different sizes and accessories fit a variety of needs. Several considerations are weight, size, and price.

You'll want to ask yourself a number of questions before deciding. Will I most often ride or walk? If you plan to walk, choose the lightest bag possible. Determine how many clubs it will have to hold. A full set or less than ten? With less than a full set, a small canvas *Sunday bag* will suffice; with more than, say, ten clubs, a larger, sturdier bag is best.

If you plan to travel with it, make sure the bag meets your needs for both clubs and accessories. Whatever bag you choose, you will have to have your own. Two players sharing a bag is another one of those things just not done.

HAND IN GLOVE

Babe Ruth never wore a batting glove; Bobby Jones never wore a golf glove. But just as every baseball player today from Little

League on up now sports one, so do most golfers. They provide a feeling of a surer grip, like batting or bowling gloves. Some putt with a glove on; others take if off. It's all a matter of personal preference.

HOW TO FIND INSTRUCTION

Dressing a good game is important to make a good impression, but it will only get you so far, even in golf. The bottom line will always be your conduct and play. For pros and duffers alike, this means lessons.

Golfers are bombarded by instruction: spoken, written, and visual. Those who seek eternal knowledge from this year's guru or superstar (coming to a book- and video store near you) soon make a disturbing discovery: not all great minds in golf think alike. In fact, they rarely agree on teaching methods, routinely contradicting each other. Moreover, instruction is often described in mystifying technical detail. It has been observed that some golf "experts" have a knack for taking an obscure subject and by explanation making it still more obscure.

The truth is that there is no magic formula. Golf requires diligence and perseverance. How else can it continue to confound even the greatest champions from one era to the next?

Fortunately, there is competent instruction readily available. Group lessons offer many advantages, not the least of which is price. They are also a great way to find people with whom to play.

Group lessons are recommended for beginners because they offer a longer lesson for a more reasonable price. Seeing others in the same boat—some better, some worse—makes lessons easier to take. They also aren't as potentially nerve-racking as private lessons. Since the pro will move up and down the line to work with students, group lessons allow opportunities to practice without an expert always looking over your shoulder.

In many areas, community schools and university continuing

education programs offer group lessons. Municipal courses, country clubs (even if you are not a member), and driving ranges can also point you in the right direction. Junior programs abound.

Finding private golf instruction is like finding a good pediatrician or dry cleaner. Ask around. Word of mouth may be your best reference. You'll find many pros have particular areas of expertise and, of course, different personalities.

The best players are not always the best coaches. Try to find a teacher, not just a good golfer. If after giving him or her a reasonable hearing, you are not comfortable with your instructor, find someone else.

HOW TO TAKE A LESSON

Besides your full set of clubs and a few dollars to pay for range balls, don't forget to bring an open mind. Improvement will be negligible without it. You may be asked to try swing techniques or practice drills that seem awkward. A changed grip will almost certainly feel uncomfortable at first. Give it all a chance; there is no quick fix. A sound swing is built in steps like a backhand in tennis or a parallel turn in skiing.

Before you start, the pro will likely want to get some sense of how far along you are. Be prepared to answer questions candidly about how often you play, what your goals are, what usually happens to your shots, and what part of your game you feel needs the most attention.

If you were going to jog, shoot a few baskets, or practice your serve, you'd warm up first; the same is true of swinging a club. Ask your instructor for a few golf stretches. A bad back will eventually dampen even the keenest enthusiasm. In golf, as in other sports, flexibility is no less important.

It may not be feasible during the course of the lesson, but before you leave, take some notes. They'll help you get your money's worth and give you something to work from later. You might also go home and practice what you learned, without a club in your hand, as a way to remind your muscles—and still preserve your lamps and vases. Golf may not be scientific, but no one denies that sound mechanics are fundamental to a sound swing.

FINDING PEOPLE TO PLAY WITH

Golfers compete largely against themselves, their own limitations, and nerves. It's the one sport, noted Robert Browning, in which "lack of skill doesn't detract from the pleasure of the game." No one tries to steal the ball, tackle you for a loss, or block your shot, reasons why golfers share a camaraderie unique in sports. Even among the professionals who battle each other every week for their livelihoods, the level of sportsmanship is high. One player commented, "It's ironic but golf encourages this sort of atmosphere of everybody pulling for each other."

Another plus is that golf doesn't require a set number of players to have a game. You can play a few holes and leave without spoiling the game, or if you're late, your partners can start without you. It doesn't matter. Golf can also be enjoyed alone.

With a *handicap*, players of different abilities can compete together fairly. It's a complicated formula. Simply, it clarifies your skill level by estimating your average strokes over par. It starts at 36 for a beginner and works down to *scratch* for an expert. Rather than asking "Are you any good?" players exchange handicaps to identify their place in the game.

Local golf associations and clubs compute and publish up-to-date handicaps, for a small fee. They also provide excellent social and competitive opportunities for every skill level. Call the pro shop of your local municipal course for more information. The ladies' associations usually have nine-hole groups for beginners or for women unable to fit in a full round.

Late afternoon is a good time to find a course at low tide.

The rates may also go down as the shadows lengthen. Even if they don't, at most courses green fees are cheaper during the week than on weekends. Charity events, routinely mentioned in the fine print of the daily sports section, offer another opportunity to find compatible players.

If you're getting started in golf, you might consider *executive courses* or *pitch and putts*, also known as *par-3 courses*. They're shorter, easier, less expensive, and take less time to play. They're a good place to get your sea legs, meet others in a less intimidating setting, and work on your short game (i.e., putting and chipping).

With the increasing popularity of golf, however, finding people to play with shouldn't be much of a problem.

TIME FOR TEE

Tee times are golf's reservation system. They're not mandatory but they are advisable, especially on weekends or holidays. Suppose you wanted to take a friend to a trendy restaurant on Friday night. You wouldn't expect to be seated immediately without first calling ahead and reserving a table. It's the same way with golf. A tee time assures your place by assigning you a specific starting time.

On a weekday afternoon you probably will not need a tee time. It's still a good idea to check in beforehand. You never know: the course could be closed, there might be a tournament, the greens might be under repair, etc. To reserve a tee time on the weekend, you will need some advance planning.

Courses differ on how—and when—they accept tee times. Every attempt to achieve equity in allotting tee times has been tried short of court-ordered lotteries.

It's not easy. The drama often begins before dawn. In worst-case situations, golfers sleep out as they might for good seats to a hot concert. At some courses we are distressed to hear that the *starter*, the person who manages the tee times, may even require a little something extra for him- or herself, in addition to the regular green fee, before allowing golfers to proceed.

A municipal course reservation system for weekend play might typically run like this: at 7 o'clock Friday morning, attendants take one tee time for the weekend over the phone and one from players waiting in line, one over the phone, one walk-up, until every slot is filled.

Private daily fee course reservations might be accepted a week in advance to play during the week, one day in advance for the weekend. As it would be at any restaurant, your reservation to play golf should be made with honorable intent. If you cannot keep it, call the pro shop with the unfortunate news, freeing up the slot for others.

When you receive a tee time, you are expected to have lined up a foursome—or at least have one assembled by your scheduled tee time. If you know someone isn't going to make it, call or alert the pro shop as soon as you can. Single golfers hang around the practice green to fill in foursomes the same way skiers wait along crowded lift lines to fill in chair lifts.

You might do the same, but be prepared to wait. A single is the low man on the totem pole. The best way to avoid being placed in an abominable fivesome is to make sure your foursome is present and accounted for. Otherwise, threesomes and two singles will be paired together.

Tee times are typically spaced eight to ten minutes apart. You will usually be given plenty of advance notice. While you're waiting, you owe it to the golfers in front of you not to crowd them on the first tee. Stay far enough back so as to be out of their perspective. Nothing can be more suffocating than standing on the first tee and looking back to see a bread line of starved golfers. Anxiously awaiting their turn (even though it may be thirty or more minutes off), they are oblivious to the disturbance they create by chatting or taking ferocious practice swings. Their time would be better spent on the practice putting green, almost always nearby, until summoned to the tee.

ANOTHER ON-TIME ARRIVAL

It should go without saying that punctuality is important to everyone's peace of mind and, thus, to playing well. We'll say it anyway because it does not happen as often as it might. One member screeching into the parking lot just as his or her group is being called to the tee is rude—plain and simple—and all too familiar. Doing so is no more conducive to good golf than running through airports is to harmonious business travel. Of course, sometimes it can't be helped; do the best you can to ensure an on-time arrival.

AT THE CLUB

They are as American as two-tone golf slacks. Country clubs were invented after the Civil War as a sort of stand-in British country estate for America's wealthy urbanites. Riding and cricket were the first attractions; it wasn't long though before golf came to dominate as its popularity spread.

Unlike the traditional British club, which provided its members with a safe refuge from their families, the country club was a place where families could recreate and socialize together, along with the "right sort of people."

Whatever country clubs have evolved into, they do remain home to many fine golf courses. The degrees of formality, pomp, or civility will vary among them. This is, after all, a place where a menu change or a new fabric pattern in the men's grillroom can inflame passions. A bill entered not long ago in the Connecticut legislature bears this out. It was aimed at broadening tee times for women (traditionally, the choice weekend slots are reserved for men). One representative who lobbied hard on the bill recalled, "I got more mail on this than on abortion." (The measure failed.)

You should be aware that if invited to someone's club for

golf, and dinner afterward, men may often need a coat and tie; women may need a skirt or dress. Some courses may prohibit blue jeans for either sex. Note the "may." Any questions can be discreetly answered in advance by calling the pro shop.

You will want to be on time. The course may not be public, but that does not mean the demand to play at private clubs is any less great. Valet service will take care of your clubs and direct you to the pro shop, locker room, or grill. Never carry your clubs into the pro shop; leave them in the stands provided outside. This goes not only for country clubs but for other courses as well. If you need to change, and locker facilities are provided, use them rather than the parking lot, even if you have to slip on just your golf shoes.

Members pay monthly dues rather than daily green fees. Everything from the bag of balls you hit on the range to your green fee to lunch will be put on a tab. Guests should be gracious about all this and plot some way of reciprocating later. Your host can advise you what an appropriate tip would be for the locker room attendant or caddy.

TAKE A HIKE

Golf was never meant to be a motor sport. While it may not be, as Mark Twain once called it, "a good walk spoiled," the Founding Fathers intended golf to be a pastoral experience. By walking, you will more fully enjoy the scenery and see the course more clearly. You'll get more exercise, save money, play faster, and make a stand for the preservation of the game, all by doing something that's good for you—walking.

On many courses, carts are now prohibited from fairways, restricted to the concrete paths. This helps preserve the course, but it necessarily keeps golfers from moving "as the crow flies" directly to their balls.

Especially for beginners, getting in and out, backing up, braking, and sharing a cart can be as challenging as the golf itself. And you've got it on good authority: there are few things more infuriating than the sound of a released cart brake during a backswing.

Everyone has gotten a few extra yards from bouncing one off the cart path, and they have made the game more accessible to the elderly, but the negatives clearly outweigh the positives.

Carts are sometimes mandatory. Many courses are designed with carts in mind, part of the arranged marriage of golf and real estate development. Longer courses mean more lots with golf course frontage. They also mean holes are placed impossibly far apart. On some courses, it seems that walking is nearly beyond the reach of all but triathletes.

Why are carts so prevalent? One word: *profit*. Carts make money. In a nation of overweight and underexercised, most of us would do well to exercise our option to walk. (Note: cart etiquette is discussed in later chapters.)

LE CADET

Caddies are making a slow and pronounced comeback, but carts nearly led to the extinction of the once venerable tradition. There was a time, not long ago, when the majority of professionals got their start in the caddy yard.

Derived from the French word *cadet*, one story holds that caddies are a legacy of none other than Mary, Queen of Scots, who naturally refused to carry her own clubs. Caddies perform many of the duties discussed in this book. They replace *divots*, attend flags, and rake *sand bunkers*. They provide the regular on-course maintenance that we find generally lacking today.

While still a bulwark of the professional tour (caddies earn a weekly salary and a percentage of their pro's earnings), most of us could play a lifetime of golf without one. This is too bad, because caddies can be an experience. Like New York cab drivers, each one has his or her own style. "In common with royalty, editors, and boxing managers," BBC commentator Henry Longhurst once noted, "the good caddie instinctively talks of 'we' and 'us'—e.g., 'We was robbed at the 14th'—instead of using the third person."

A good caddy also has a bit of amateur psychologist in him. Skip Daniels, who shepherded Gene Sarazen to a British Open championship, "knew instinctively how to inspire his man with confidence." Their story, "My Favorite Caddy," remains a wonderful and entertaining tribute.

Of course, caddies can inspire something other than confidence. There is, for instance, the old joke that has the golfer asking his caddy, "What do I need to get *home* (to the green)?"

"Mister," replied the caddy, "I don't even know where you live." Or the Scottish caddy who, when asked by his golfer, "Can I get home with a five-iron?" laconically answered, "Eventually."

If you have the opportunity and the means, securing a caddy can be a real treat. No bag or cart to worry about, someone to find your errant shots, and expertise of the course at the ready. Everyone who plays in Scotland always comes home with a few caddy stories. A tip will be in order if he or she has performed the job to your satisfaction. The pro shop can advise you on this account, if you have any questions.

Before we set out to play, with the basics of attire, equipment, and instruction behind us, the quest turns first to practice, and for most of us that means a visit to the driving range.

CHAPTER ONE CHECKLIST

Attire
__ Call the pro shop if you have any questions about attire.
__ Classic dress for men: slacks, collared sport shirt, golf shoes.

___ Classic dress for women: knee-lengthed skirt, collared sport shirt, golf shoes.
___ A wide-brimmed hat, a visor, a bandanna, and sunscreen are fashionable preventives for skin cancer.
___ At clubs, use available locker facilities.
___ Golf or tennis shoes, please.

Equipment
___ A good swing can hit any club.
___ Good used clubs are readily available.
___ Take a 'test drive.'
___ X-outs are an honest bargain.
___ Is your bag for walking or riding?
___ Ranges, munis, private clubs, and adult-ed programs may offer group lessons.

Getting Started
___ Play the course at low tide: weekday afternoons.
___ Par-3 and executive courses won't take all day.
___ Call for a tee time and be prompt.
___ Call and cancel if you can't keep it.
___ Never carry your clubs into the pro shop.
___ You must have your own bag; no sharing.

CHAPTER ONE GLOSSARY

Address—Position or stance before the swing.

Balata ball—With liquid center designed for faster swing speeds. Has soft pliable cover that offers more control but is easier to cut, as it magnifies imperfections in the swing. Favored by professionals.

Cavity-backed Designs—Refers to the distribution of weight on an iron. Designed to provide a larger sweet spot by weighting the club on the outside or perimeter of the club head. Also known as perimeter weighted.

Divots—Turf cut by swinging the club.

Executive Course—Shorter in distance to allow for faster play, but longer than a pitch and putt.

Handicap—System used to allow golfers of any skill level to compete together fairly. Recognized internationally, it identifies a player's skill level.

Home—Slang for the green.

In Regulation—Statistic that signifies the ideal number of strokes required to reach the green before putting. On a par-4 hole, two shots would be required to reach the green; on a par-3, one shot.

Municipal/Public Course—Owned and operated by city or county government. Open to the public with few, if any, restrictions.

PGA Tour—The Professional Golfers Association tournament circuit. Players must attend qualifying (or Q school) to obtain their "card," which allows them to play the tour for one year.

Pitch and Putt—Usually a nine-hole course, each hole a par-3.

Plus fours—Style of knickers popularized by 1920s golfers. Named for the additional amount of fabric draped over the knee.

Private Daily Fee Course—Privately owned, but also open to the public. May charge slightly higher green fees and have some dress restrictions.

Radiused Sole—Arc or curve on the bottom of an iron club.

Sand Bunkers—Also known as sand traps.

Scratch—An even-par score. A scratch player has a zero handicap.

Starter—Course employee in charge of tee times.

Sunday Bag—Designed to carry fewer clubs than larger bags.

Surlyn ball—Solid center, harder cover, a more durable ball, appropriate for the overwhelming majority of golfers.

Touring Pro—A professional tournament player, as opposed to a teaching or club PGA pro.

X-out balls—Discount balls due to factory overruns or cosmetic blemishes. A good buy.

AT HOME ON THE RANGE

GOLF'S LABORATORY

THE DRIVING RANGE is golf's laboratory, a place to practice and experiment. One glance at the various works in progress reveals a basic truth: there is more than one way to hit a golf ball. Just as each of us has his or her own distinctive walk, it seems that no two golfers swing exactly the same way. Watch the touring pros on the range before a tournament and you will see this confirmed even at the game's highest levels.

Ranges can be raked pastures, indoor domes, triple-deckered tiers, or even subterranean netted cages with computer graphics. Some offer memberships. Others charge a set fee for as many balls as you can hit in a half hour. The usual fee is per bucket or bag. Many ranges also rent clubs, some specifically made for range use (i.e., reinforced to take a beating). They also offer instruction.

HELLO, MY NAME IS

Before you take your clubs out to practice or play, it's a good idea to label them. Doing so might prevent a loss on the range, on the practice green, or on the course. In every pro shop orphaned clubs gather dust behind the counter. And somewhere, someone is looking for their 9-iron.

ALL DOWN THE LINE

Whatever type of practice area you use (and an empty field can serve very nicely), proper etiquette means using the facility safely. Most ranges outline a specific hitting area. On grass ranges this is typically done with stakes or ground ropes several feet apart. Always hit from between the ropes and/or stakes. This allows grass to grow back on fallow sections of the hitting area, and more important, it helps establish an even hitting line.

Take a little extra precaution, nevertheless. Before getting down to business, make sure you line up evenly with the golfers on either side of you. If you don't, you're taking the chance that someone might get hit.

HITTING WHERE THE GRASS IS GREENER

If you're willing to walk to the far end of the range, you'll often find the hitting surface, either grass or artificial turf mats, in better condition than nearer the cash register. You'll also further distance yourself from distractions. Something else to look out for: the ropes or stakes are not always lined up evenly with the lay of the land. They can be inaccurate guides, with the result that your *alignment*—and subsequently your shots—will be led astray by the illusion created. The rope can also be a painful distraction if caught with the full might of a swing. Be sure to set up far enough behind it.

CREATE SOME SPACE

Always position your clubs well behind you, either on the ground or in the stand provided. Make sure you've got enough elbow-room without having to worry about what's happening around you. Place your bucket of balls in front so they will be close enough to gather but far enough away to avoid potential ri-

Stakes or ropes can be inaccurate guides for alignment.

cochets. This will also save you from reaching back into a neighbor's line of fire.

Range balls are not the same as the balls in your bag, no matter what brand you play. The average range ball is built with lower compression, which simply means that it does not travel as far as other balls do. This makes them easier to collect and

Proper range set-up.

less attractive to thieves. So if your shots all seem short, don't despair. On most driving ranges, distances are far from precise.

BEAT THE CLOCK?

Speed of play is important on the course, but there are no rewards for hitting a bucket of range balls the fastest. Take your time. Strive for quality, not quantity.

To make practice more meaningful, don't hesitate to improve your *lie*, the position of the ball on the ground. Tee up the ball, especially if the grass or mat has been worn bare and doesn't provide much cushion from which to hit. In an actual round these would be violations of the Rules of Golf, but this not an actual round, it's practice.

Take an enlightened approach to your mis-hits. Even in batting practice, the greats foul some off. Of course, in golf, unlike baseball, you have to play your foul balls, but on the range, finding the balls is someone else's concern. Put the bad shots out of your mind and go back to work on consistency and accuracy.

YOU MAY FIRE WHEN READY

You will often see golfers on the range blasting as many balls as fast and as far as they can with little regard for accuracy. While it may be good fun, it certainly doesn't make for good golf. Distance alone is not a nonstop ticket to the top of tournament *leader boards*. As Harvey Penick said, "The woods are full of long hitters."

The driving range reveals some insight into a golfer's personality. Better golfers studiously go about their business. Inconsiderate golfers who swing out of control, without purpose, sometimes create unnecessary disturbances. The driving range is not a library, but it is a laboratory, and people are trying to accomplish something.

THE SHORT GAME

The majority of shots during a round will be played from 100 yards or less (including putting). That's where the real *scoring* is done. Rather than blasting away, the better players concentrate on the *short game*, loosening up with the *short irons* before moving through the bag to practice with *longer* clubs. J. H. Taylor, one of England's finest players in the early part of the twentieth century, noted that "most amateurs practice driving. Most pros practice approaching." Nothing's changed.

Whatever you're working on, dividing your balls into smaller

piles will help keep you from falling into an indiscriminate blasting pattern. Before you swing, pick out a target. Treat each ball
like a real shot. That way, once you get out on the course, the
fairways won't seem so narrow compared with the wide vista
of the range.

Each golfer brings a different level of ability and experience
to the driving range, a melting pot where experts toil alongside
duffers. Rome wasn't built in a day; neither was a sound golf
swing. Forbearance and patience are essential. Remember, there
will always be someone who seems to be doing better or worse
than you. Unfortunately, one or the other (probably both) will
want to give you advice.

HUMAN HAZARD #1

The old maxim that many receive advice but few profit by it is
certainly true in golf, especially on the range. Advice has rami-
fications during actual play. These are discussed in later chapters.
There is always time on the driving range for an uninhibited
give-and-take about the swing. This general exchange of ideas
is very much a part of the game.

Often, however, the advice, while well intentioned, gets too
personal. It can easily become an annoyance, especially for beginners, as inevitable as it is unwanted.

Harvey Penick believed that a promising Japanese player
pursuing her game in the United States owed much of her rapid
improvement to the fact that she didn't understand English; thus
no one could confuse her with contradictory advice.

There is an appropriate response for someone who seems
too forthcoming. It is: "Thank you very much. I'll certainly
consider your suggestions." If you had a severe toothache, would
you consult the man on the street or a dentist? As with an
overbite, successful diagnosis and treatment of your swing is best
left to professionals.

One of the wonderful advantages of taking lessons is that it fortifies you against the flurry of tips and suggestions that swirl through golf. There is one long-standing rule governing advice: The only time it should be offered is when someone requests it. If only it were adhered to.

TIDYING UP

Before you put your clubs away, be sure to clean them, or at least wipe them off. Facilities of some kind are often provided at ranges. There may be a bucket of soapy water and a brush, a club cleaner set up behind the hitting stations, or a mechanical unit set beside the pro shop. For the optimum use of your clubs, before you throw your bag in the trunk, avail yourself of whatever facilities are offered. And since you're putting them in the trunk, you should know that extremes in temperature, particularly heat, can adversely affect the adhesives that secure grips and club heads to the shaft.

ON THE PRACTICE GREEN

Harvey Penick had a way of emphasizing the importance of putting practice. He'd point to a crowded range, then look back at the people putting on the practice green and say, "These people [on the green] are going to take their money." Even if you're not putting for dough, diligence on the practice green is usually rewarded with lower scores.

In baseball, a fly ball caught at the fence counts the same as a pop fly to the catcher: one out. It's the same with golf. The inescapable truth is that a missed eighteen-inch putt counts the same as a 270-yard drive: one stroke. The buck in golf stops on the putting green. A cursory glance at history reveals that all great golfers have been great putters: put another way, there are no great golfers who haven't been great putters.

Practice greens at courses are usually free and open to the public. Golfers share an affinity with fishermen who always keep their gear close at hand; their putter is never far off. You'll often see people slipping in a few putts at lunch or on their way home from work dressed for the office.

Golf attire is not required to use a practice green; proper shoes are. Don't step on a green without them. Actually, it's a good idea to stay off the green unless you are putting. Walk around rather than cross over on your way to the clubhouse, pro shop, or car.

The practice green differs in several respects from the greens on the course, but the etiquette considerations are the same. Chapter 7 is devoted to comportment on greens during a round.

Several holes are cut into a practice green to accommodate many golfers at once. It can get crowded, but there is no reason why they can't be comfortably shared with a little consideration.

As you might expect, loud or boisterous behavior will not

Standing too close to another hole on the practice green.

be appreciated. A practice putt sunk from downtown does not merit a celebratory lap exchanging high-fives.

More than one person can putt to the same hole. It is discourteous, however, to tie up a hole that you're not using. This can easily be done without thinking. After you've retrieved your ball, move far enough away from the hole you've finished so others have a clear shot. One golfer, oblivious to others around him, can tie up two, even three holes at once.

A packed practice green still has empty usable space. Move to an area of the green that doesn't have a hole cut in it and you'll be able to putt in peace. Practice *touch and feel*, gauging how hard a stroke it takes to sink a three-, four-, or five-foot putt. Or putt two or three balls in clusters. As is true with the greens on the course, practice green holes are regularly rotated to offer different putts from one day to the next.

Go ahead and hit some long putts (sixty to seventy footers) if the practice green is empty. When it is crowded, courtesy insists that you shoot from closer range (fifteen to twenty feet or less).

GEOMETRY REVIEW

Time for a little high school geometry. You may recall that a line is the straightest distance between two points. What does this have to do with etiquette on the green? Plenty. If ever a top ten list was compiled of reasons why good golfers don't like to play with inexperienced golfers, stepping on *putting lines* would top the list.

There exists an imaginary line that connects every ball on the green to the hole. These lines are known as putting lines. The putting line, in other words, is the path that a ball will likely travel en route to the hole. Your mission is to walk to, and putt, your ball without stepping on someone else's line.

What's the big deal about stepping on someone's putting line? Believe it or not, your footprint, as light as Fred Astaire's or Ginger Rogers', might cause a depression in the green that

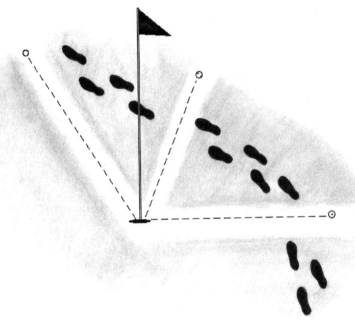

Walk to your ball and putt without stepping on someone else's "line."

would deflect a ball from rolling into the cup. It is one of those courtesies that sets golf apart from other sports and, incidentally, sets golfers who observe it apart from golfers who don't. Sportsmanship demands that your opponent or partner be given the best opportunity to sink the putt without human interference. Then, if he misses, the fault rightfully rests where it belongs.

We don't want you to feel as if you are negotiating a minefield. Avoiding someone's line on a crowded practice green might even pose a challenge for Fred or Ginger. Just be aware of the lines and do the best you can.

Putting lines are more significant when strokes are at stake during actual play. But the practice green remains not only a good place to practice putting; it's also a good place to practice etiquette.

PUTTING PRACTICE

The range blaster has an equivalent on the practice putting green, and he's just as ill-served. You'll often see golfers practice the same putt over and over again, the balls stacking up around the hole. The problem is, in golf, there are no do-overs, no second chances. You will never get three turns to sink the same putt. So why practice it? If you miss, that's a different story. Then you're faced with a completely new putt.

Practice as if each putt counted, as it does on the course. With one ball, move around the green, from one hole to the next. Try and *two-putt* or better. Playing this way also frees up holes for others.

BEFORE THE WINDUP AND THE PITCH

Pitching or *chipping* from off the green may be expressly prohibited on practice greens. Look for a sign posted around the green. Some courses set aside a green to practice approach shots from 100 yards or less. These can similarly be shared; several people hitting from different distances. Make sure your balls are indelibly marked before you hit so you can identify them on the green. Since there is no supervision or standard hitting line as you'd find on a range, before you start practicing, be sure you will not endanger or disturb others.

If pitching or chipping is allowed on a practice putting green, shoot for the holes closest to you. When the green is empty, it's safe to play to the holes on the far side of the green, but not when it might distract others.

Be especially careful retrieving your approach shots from the green. It's very easy to catch and scar the surface with an iron,

Don't gouge the putting surface with your putter or an iron.

gouging it like tearing the baize of a pool table with a cue. Pick the balls up or gently push them along with the club. Do not take a full, or even a casual, swing or passing swipe with a club of any kind on the green.

KEEP OFF THE GRASS

Practice greens can keep irregular hours. Greens are very expensive and require staggering amounts of money to build and maintain. They are especially susceptible to the vagaries of weather. Heavy rains, turf blight, or routine maintenance all might result in their closing (while the course may still remain open). If the sign says Closed, stay off, even if the green looks inviting.

THE FLAG

Careless treatment of the flagstick can damage the fragile area around the cup on a practice green just as easily as it can on the course. Be gentle pulling it out; don't yank it. And of course, walk softly on the green. Never run. Always pick up your feet to avoid leaving cleat marks from dragging spikes.

PUTTERING

Greens come in many shapes and sizes. Some resemble states, hearts, cartoon characters, etc. There are many more subtle differences. Various strains of grass differ from region to region, and each has different characteristics that affect the roll of a ball. As you probably already know, golfers can spend hours talking about green conditions. Some common varieties and their general characteristics are noted in the end of the chapter glossary.

When people say a green is *fast*, they mean the ball does not take as much effort or energy to start and keep it rolling. On a *slow* green, the converse is true. The ball has to be struck harder to cover the same distance.

The *grain* of the grass also affects putts. The art of judging what a putted ball will do is known as *reading* the green. A ball traveling with the grain will roll faster and farther than a ball rolling against it.

FYI

Instruction books continue to dominate the dreams, the thoughts, and, consequently, the libraries of golfers. There is a dizzying array of titles and promises. Some even make good reading. Chapter 9 includes some recommendations.

One tip for southpaws: instruction books and videos are almost exclusively demonstrated by right-handed golfers. If you look at them in a mirror, however, you will see the shot executed from your perspective. (We tried it—it works!)

A sense of perspective may also be necessary when it comes to deciphering the Rules of Golf. But while they may seem as complex as an IRS form, the rules need not be quite so taxing to the novice golfer—as we'll see in the next chapter.

CHAPTER TWO CHECKLIST

__ Label your clubs.

At Home on the Range
__ Line up evenly with golfers on either side.
__ Beware of inaccurate alignment from ropes, stakes, etc.
__ Create some space between you and other golfers.
__ Resist temptation to blast away.
__ Feel free to tee up your ball. This is practice, not play.
__ "Most amateurs practice driving. Most pros practice approaching."
__ Steer clear of "helpful" hints.

At Home on the Green
__ Stay off the green unless putting. Walk around.
__ No high-fives.
__ Move away from one hole before putting to another.
__ Putt with one ball.
__ Rotate between holes instead of camping out at one.
__ Pick up your feet to avoid scarring the green.

CHAPTER TWO GLOSSARY

Alignment—Body and club face position at address in relation to the target.

Chip—A low, short approach shot to the green.

Fast Green vs. Slow Green—Fast greens are slick in relation to the stroke needed to roll the ball over the green. Slow putts require a harder stroke to cover the same ground.

Grain—The angle the grass grows. The roll of a putted ball is determined in part by the direction of the grass blades. A putt with the grain will roll faster than one struck against the grain.

Leader Board—Scoreboard that tabulates ranking of players during a tournament.

Lie—Position of the ball on the ground, or the angle of the club head to the shaft.

Long Irons—The 1-, 2-, 3-, and 4-irons.

Pitch—A high, short approach shot to the green.

Putting Lines—The line the ball will travel to the hole on the green. A golfer lining up his or her putt is estimating the distance and line of the putt.

Reading a Putt—The ability to interpret the speed and contour of a green before putting.

Scoring—Colloquial term for shooting low scores. Also refers to markings on the face of a club.

Short Game—Approaching and putting. A separate game within golf that begins approximately 100 yards from the hole.

Short Irons— The 7-, 8-, and 9-iron, pitching wedge, and sand wedge.

Touch and Feel—The ability to judge distances accurately and putt with delicacy.

Two-Putt—Taking two putts to complete the hole.

3
A 1040EZ FOR GOLFERS

THE RULES OF Etiquette are not really rules, merely suggestions that complement the official Rules of Golf. The two are closely interwoven, nevertheless. A violation of one often violates the spirit or intent of the other. Both protect the integrity of the game. Playing by the rules is simply considered good etiquette.

The very nature of golf makes it different from other sports. From a practical perspective, it would be impossible to officiate the game any other way than by relying on the morals of its players. Unlike other sports, golf is not played "between the lines" but over hundreds of acres. Consider a tennis court or a soccer field in comparison. Each conforms to dimensions the same the world over. But every golf course is different, with its own dimensions, flavor, character. Clearly, the Rules of Golf have a lot of ground to cover. And not just literally.

The rules preside not only over every golf course, tundra to tropics, but over every golfer as well, duffer to professional. If they daunt the average player, in part it's because they are so comprehensive. And if they read as if written for someone else, it's true. They are. The rules cover a variety of competitions and must offer guidance for a cornucopia of predicaments unimaginable in other sports. Balls have been impaled on barbed wire, landed in back pockets and trouser cuffs, on alligator tails, in bird nests, etc.

For the recreational player, the Rules of Golf are akin to the common-sense rules of the road. Speed limits were established in the best interests of all drivers, just as the Rules of Golf were established in the best interests of all golfers. But what driver hasn't exceeded a speed limit when the road was empty?

So it also is with golf. During casual play, lies are improved, *gimmes* assumed. In practice rounds or a few holes at dusk, liberties can be safely taken. The danger is that once the barrier is broken and the rules are casually discarded, the herd begins to roam at will. In recreational play, the rules are there for each of us to observe or neglect, a personal decision based upon consideration of the situation.

In tournament play, there is no middle ground. Players are responsible for knowing and following the rules. Where other sports rely on policing teams of officials and the unblinking eye of the camera, golfers referee themselves. It's a responsibility uncommon in sport, extending all the way from local events to the U.S. Open. Adherence to this code is universal. Golfers routinely call themselves for infractions, putting the best interests of the game above all else.

When a self-imposed penalty cost Bobby Jones the 1925 U.S. Open, his response was characteristic: "That's just the way the game is played"—and must be played to ensure fairness. The rules have helped keep professional golf judiciously clean for the most part from the controversies that have wracked other sports. For that alone they should be respected.

To the recreational player, the rules may seem foreign and incredibly exhaustive. Too few golfers recognize, however, that the rules exist as much to help as to penalize.

Like etiquette, the rules also present another line of demarcation that distinguishes golfers who know and observe them from golfers who don't take the time to learn or couldn't care less. Feeling comfortable in any situation comes in part from knowing you are doing the right thing. Even if you don't always adhere to them, if you at least have a working knowledge of the rules, an important aspect of golf will be less mysterious.

It has often been said that there are three kinds of golf: golf, tournament golf, and major championship golf. Having made our pitch for the rules, if you play golf, in the interests of time or in consideration of others, strict adherence is not imperative. Beginners should not feel obligated or pressured to keep score, documenting each . . . and . . . every . . . single . . . stroke. The self-inflicted torture of repeated miscues from impossible situations will not raise the level of your game, only your blood pressure.

Once a hole has lost its appeal, it's OK, even advisable, to *pick up*. Your playing partners will offer a silent prayer of thanks for your consideration. See if they don't cheer your next good shot enthusiastically. Playing out each hole, come hell or high water, can make for a very long and unpleasant experience for everyone. If your score on a hole has reached double digits, if everyone else in your foursome has *holed out* and is waiting, along with several groups behind you—then, to borrow a phrase: know when to say when. In tournament play, of course, there is no picking up ever. The only escape is withdrawal from the field and disqualification.

Another good reason to know the rules is so you won't have to ask someone else. Repeated consultations slow down the game and, as the round wears on, will become increasingly less welcome. Everyone has enough to think about with their own game.

On the other hand, do not feel that you owe it to others and to golf itself to wear the mantle of rules custodian, rampantly dispensing unsolicited interpretations or remarking upon the breaches of others. You can play by the rules. You should, but no one will bat an eyelash if you don't. What someone else does during casual play is their business.

Joe Dey, executive director of the USGA for 35 years, was once asked how he handled rules violations during a recreational round. "If it's serious," he said, "I usually won't say anything then; I may tell them in the locker room later. We don't make a thing of it." Under similar circumstances, there's no reason why you should either.

To help golfers with their understanding of the rules, in addition to the official *Rules of Golf* (updated annually), the USGA also publishes *Golf Rules in Pictures*, available in most bookstores.

We encourage golfers to purchase AND read the rules. The book is small enough to carry in your golf bag. To make them more palatable and less intimidating, we offer an arbitrary short form of frequently encountered situations and the appropriate

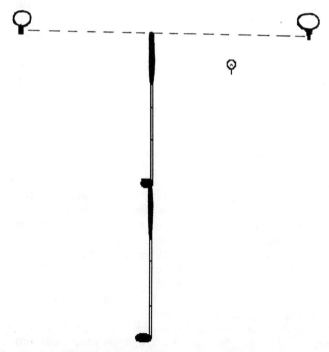

You can tee off from a maximum of two club lengths behind the markers.

rules that come into play. These are by no means complete. They will, however, get you started.

A 1040EZ SHORT FORM OF THE RULES OF GOLF

1) Tee Off Between the Markers

On every *teeing ground*, the place where each hole begins, markers define the area from which the ball must be played. They may be wooden blocks, stone carvings or colored plastic balls. The rule is your ball must NEVER be teed up in front of the markers. You are, however, allowed to play from behind the markers within two club lengths.

Tee markers are moved periodically to allow sections of the teeing ground to grow back. Rotating the markers forward or back a few yards necessarily affects the length of the hole. On any given day, a hole might play longer or shorter than it did the day before, and differ slightly from the yardage printed on the card or posted on a nearby sign.

2) Play the Ball as It Lies

From the tee until you reach the green, you should not improve the lie of your ball. You should not bend, break, or move anything that is growing or attached. You may move (UNAT-TACHED) limbs, rocks, leaves, and so on. Mark and lift a ball for the purposes of identification anywhere except in a hazard, where it cannot be lifted but must be played as it lies. Play the course as you find it.

Winter rules are a notable exception when course conditions are adversely affected by weather, construction, and seasonal maintenance. In colder regions, winter rules may be an option from November through February. They are, however, a tempting crutch in any season.

Winter rules allow golfers, in the guise of fairness or to protect the course, to move their ball to better ground and a preferred lie. Former president Richard Nixon allegedly played them year-round. Tommy Armour, the famous pro and teacher, however, counseled against them as a bad habit.

3) A Whiff Is the Same as a Strike

When you swing and miss in baseball, it counts as a strike against you. Same thing in golf. Called a *whiff* (or a fan), it always counts as one stroke added to your score. It can happen to anybody. If you whiff, treat it matter-of-factly. The less time spent with the frustration or amusement of the miss, the less time wasted. It's been said many times: the most important shot in golf is the next shot. A corollary rule is the simple precept that the ball cannot be advanced without striking it. (Note: If you knock your ball off the tee at address, or it falls off the tee, it does not count as a stroke against you. Simply retee the ball and hit it.)

4) Out-of-Bounds—Lost Ball

White stakes set in the ground along fairways define out-of-bounds (commonly known as OB). OB keeps golfers, never shy of a challenge, from going to extremes in the pursuit of par, playing off neighboring pool decks or living room rugs, etc. Playing the ball as it lies is a good rule of thumb when the ball is within the confines of the course but not when it lies out-of-bounds.

When a ball is observed going OB, the golfer will drop another ball and play from the same spot. The penalty is one stroke. The way to calculate it is: one (for the original shot that went OB), two (for the penalty), and three (for the new shot from the same place).

The rules do not allow you to drop a new ball at the approximate spot where the first ball was lost or went out-of-bounds. Golfers do it all the time in recreational golf or in the interests of speeding up play. This is fine but should never be done in tournaments, including charity and social events. The rules exist to preserve the game for the field, ensuring that everyone plays by the same code.

5) Provisionals

If you think your ball may be lost or OB, announce and hit a *provisional*, a second ball from the same spot. On the tee, wait until everyone else has teed off.

It's insurance. If you can find your original shot, simply pick up the provisional and play on with your first ball. No penalty. If you can't find your initial shot, however, you must play the provisional and incur a penalty stroke.

If your tee shot goes OB and you hit a provisional, you'll be playing your fourth shot from the fairway. Your score would count one stroke (for the original shot), two (for the penalty), and three (for your tee shot). (Note: You are allowed to keep hitting the provisional until it reaches the estimated distance of the original ball, but each stroke counts if you can't find your first ball and end up having to complete the hole with the provisional. If you do find your original ball in bounds, you must play out the hole with it. The penalty stroke, and all strokes, with the provisional ball don't count.)

6) Unplayable Lies

You decide when and if your ball is unplayable (under rocks, buried in tall grass, etc.) Rather than risk damaging a club or wasting several strokes, discretion may be the better part of valor. For the cost of a penalty stroke, you may move the ball two club lengths in any direction (extricating yourself to a better place to hit) so long as the ball is not moved closer to the hole.

This may not seem like much of a bargain, but every golfer learns through hindsight, when the ball remains unmoved after several swings, that it can be a wise decision. There are two other options. You can return to the original scene of the unfortunate shot and hit another ball. Penalty: one stroke. Or you may retreat on a line as far as you like, keeping the spot where the ball lies, between you and the hole. Penalty: one stroke. This rule may be invoked anywhere on the course except when the ball rests in a water hazard. In a bunker, you have the same options: 1) return to play from the site of the previous shot, 2) stay inside

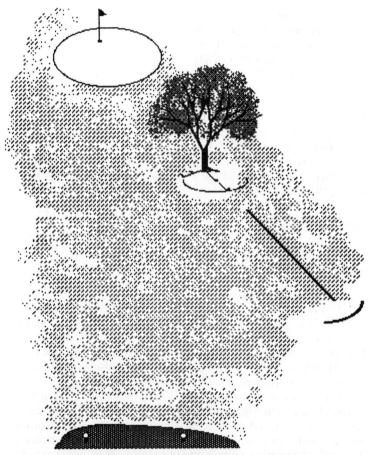

You have three options with an unplayable line: a) Go back to the tee; b) Move two club lengths and drop—but no closer to the hole; c) Retreat on a line, keeping the spot where the ball lies between you and the hole.

the bunker, moving no closer to the hole, and drop within two club lengths, or 3) move back on a line as long as you stay in the bunker. Penalty: one stroke.

7) R-e-l-i-e-f

Finally, a rule that doesn't cost a stroke. You are entitled to relief, also known as a *free drop*, when your ball comes to rest on a cart path, in *casual water* (standing water from rain or sprinklers), on an anthill, on a sprinkler head, or is interfered with by any man-made object: water fountains, distance markers, benches, whatever. (One exception: out-of-bounds markers are considered permanent fixtures of the course. No relief is given. You'll have to hit around them.)

To take relief, you first have to find the *nearest point of relief*. It is the spot as near as possible to the original position of the ball, no closer to the hole that will not interfere with your swing or stance. Drop within one club length of that point. This rule also applies when you cannot take a proper stance because of a sprinkler head, bench, cart path, etc. You cannot take relief just because an obstruction or a tree is in your path, only if a man-made object interferes with your stance or swing. The same relief is offered for *ground under repair*.

8) Hazards

A *hazard* is a bunker (commonly called a sand trap), a *water hazard*, or a *lateral water hazard*. Nowhere on the course are golfers allowed to remove, bend, or break anything, fixed or growing, to improve their shot. In a hazard, no *loose impediments* (sticks, leaves, grass, etc.) may be removed. Any movable obstructions (cans, bottles, and other man-made objects), however, may be removed. You are not allowed to mark or lift your ball to identify it. There is no penalty for playing the wrong ball from a hazard, but you must not complete the hole with the wrong ball.

One rule that applies to all hazards without exception: You

may not ground your club in a hazard, that is, touch the ground with your club until you actually swing.

A water hazard is any sea, lake, pond, river, ditch . . . or other open water course. They are marked with yellow stakes or lines painted on the banks and include the ground inside the markings. If your ball comes to rest in the water or inside the stakes or lines, you may go back to the previous hitting area and hit again. Penalty: one stroke.

Another choice is to walk back and hit from behind the hazard. On a line with the flagstick and the point the ball entered the water, you may go back as far as you like to find a good spot from which to play. Penalty: one stroke. Playing at Pebble Beach, Arnold Palmer once hit his ball into the Pacific Ocean. The joke was he'd have to go to Hawaii to find the closest point of relief.

A lateral water hazard runs parallel to the fairway, defined by red stakes or lines. After a ball has entered a lateral hazard, you may drop a ball two club lengths from where the ball *crossed the margin*, or boundary, of the hazard. Penalty: one stroke. You may find it advantageous to pick your position on either side of the hazard, which is perfectly acceptable.

A player is allowed to hit a ball resting in shallow water. You can even wade into the water. Remember not to *ground your club* by touching the surface or any other part of the hazard before playing. Then swing away. To advance the ball, you can hit anything you want. Have fun.

9) On the Putting Green
It is a two-stroke penalty to strike another player's ball or the flagstick when putting on the green. There is nothing wrong, however, with hitting someone's ball on the green when you are playing from off the green.

When one ball hits another, on either the fairway or the green, simply replace the ball hit to its approximate original position. It is each player's responsibility to make sure the flagstick is removed and balls are marked on the green to avoid a penalty. (Note: If your ball lands on the wrong putting green, that is, a hole you are not playing, simply take the nearest point of relief and play on. No penalty.)

10) Local Rules

The rules do cover a lot of ground, but with golf played as enthusiastically over desert and tundra as it is over Bermuda and bent grass, there are exceptions. Local rules cover those exceptions peculiar to individual courses. You'll find them listed on the back of scorecards, posted in the pro shop, or designated by signs on the course. They commonly come into play on holes over water. After you hit a couple into the drink, local rules may allow you to carry your ball across and play on from dry land.

11) Advice

We've discussed advice on the practice range, but this is advice of a different sort. The rules allow you to ask questions about anything on the course: distance, hidden hazards, impending trouble on *blind holes*, anything you want—with one notable exception. In tournament play it is against the rules to ask what club someone else used to hit their shot. You can go over and look but not ask. In recreational play, this goes on all the time, but if you are playing with strangers or more experienced players and want to make a good impression, keep your curiosity to yourself.

As your proficiency at golf improves, so should your knowledge of the rules. "If Golfers play fair," wrote author Geoffrey Cousins, "they need not fear the Rules." That's pretty easy to remember.

CHAPTER THREE CHECKLIST

— Playing by the Rules of Golf is good etiquette.
— In tournaments, all players are responsible for following the rules.
— Know the rules so you won't have to ask someone else.
— Bending the rules is a personal choice in casual play.
— Play the course as you find it.
— You decide when and if your ball is unplayable.
— In a hazard you may not remove loose impediments.
— You may not ground your club in a hazard.
— Rules change on the putting green.
— Know the following:
    —Out-of-Bounds   —Lost Ball
    —Unplayable Lie   —Rules in Hazards

CHAPTER THREE GLOSSARY

Blind Hole—Hole where because of its topography the golfer is unable to see where the ball will land.

Casual Water—Accumulation of water on the course that is not normally part of the course. Standing water from sprinklers is casual water.

Crossed the Margin—Used to describe the point where a ball crosses the boundary line of a hazard.

Free Drop—Slang for allowance to move the ball to a better position without penalty.

Gimme—Slang for a conceded putt. Same as "that's good" or "inside the leather."

Ground Under Repair—Portion of the course undergoing maintenance.

Ground Your Club—To touch the ground with the club. A penalty inside a hazard.

Hazard—A ditch, stream, pond, lake, or bunker on the golf course.

Hole Out—To stroke the final putt into the cup.

Lateral Water Hazard—Any water hazard that runs parallel to the hole. Defined by red lines or stakes.

Loose Impediments—Unattached natural objects (grass, leaves, twigs, etc.) that are not fixed or growing. May be removed anywhere EXCEPT inside a hazard.

Nearest Point of Relief—The point no nearer the hole that is the closest point where relief may be taken.

Obstructions—Man-made objects such as benches, water fountains, cans, bottles, cart paths, etc.

Pick Up—Literally picking up a ball before the hole is completed. A timesaver in recreational play; in tournament play, it implies withdrawal or automatic disqualification.

Provisional—A ball played in the event of a lost ball or one suspected of being out-of-bounds. It is played after the errant shot and becomes the ball in play if the original ball is lost or OB.

Teeing Ground—The starting place for a hole.

Water Hazard—As defined by the USGA: "Any sea, lake, pond, river, ditch, surface drainage ditch, or other open water course (regardless of whether or not it contains water), and anything of a similar nature." Defined by yellow lines or stakes.

Whiff—To swing and completely miss the ball. Counts as one stroke. Also: fan.

Winter Rules—Local rules played in off-season to protect the course; allows liberties, such as moving ball to a better lie otherwise not allowed.

TEEING OFF

GRIDLOCK ON THE GOLF COURSE

A SIGN AT a venerable Scottish course advises: A Round of Golf Should Not Require More than Three Hours. Elsewhere, unfortunately, that's more than a wee bit wistful. Four hours plus has become the norm; on weekends, closer to five hours, sometimes longer.

The number one complaint in golf is not that it's too expensive or too difficult but that it takes too long to play. Aside from the president, a few hardy "dawn patrol" golfers, and an occasional millionaire, the problem is so pervasive that no golfer can be said to be immune from the ravages of stop-and-go traffic known as slow play. Under its weight, author John Updike noted: "The old courtesies implode in the crush. . . . The course isn't just overplayed, it's pillaged."

The bad news is that as golf continues to prosper, slow play gets worse. There is some good news. Slow play is not terminal. In fact, an effective and painless remedy already exists and has been on the books for years. The antidote can be administered by any golfer who cares about the game. It has shown impressive results in field tests alleviating the pain caused by slow play. In time, large-scale immunization may eradicate the blight altogether.

The cure is twofold: 1) play in a timely manner; 2) practice the traditional courtesies of the course. These simple precepts offer the best approach to eliminating slow play. And both are a heck of a lot easier to take than on-course time clocks, five-somes, and other less attractive alternatives.

BE PREPARED

The first tee sets the pace for the round, so it is imperative to get off to a good start. Like a stalled vehicle that backs up a freeway for miles, the slowest player on a golf course imposes his or her pace on everyone who follows.

As you wait to tee off, take inventory. Have enough balls? A scorecard? Enough tees? A ball-mark repair tool and ball marker? Your putter? Be certain. Knowing you're ready has a way of fortifying self-confidence. You don't have to be a leading money winner on the Tour to know that running back to the range or the car, while everyone waits on the first tee, is not conducive to good golf. It's also embarrassing.

Little things, like always carrying two balls in your pocket in the event of misfortune or taking more than one club with you onto the tee box (if you're uncertain about which club to hit) can save time. Multiply a few minutes wasted by other foursomes over eighteen holes on any given Saturday morning and slow play becomes less mysterious. It starts on the first tee.

Whether you intend to keep score or not, it is a good idea to carry a scorecard. A map is printed on the back. It also supplies other valuable pointers. Yardage to the hole from various points of the fairway, par for each hole, local rules, and a comparison rating for handicap purposes are all on there somewhere. Score-cards also make nice souvenirs. Don't leave for the first tee without it.

RED, WHITE, OR BLUE

Beginning skiers quickly learn to keep to the trails marked by green circles. These trails are tailored to their skill levels, generously wide and not too steep. Blue squares mark the intermediate slopes; black diamonds designate the advanced slopes, with names such as Nose Bleed or Mine Shaft, lest there be any doubt that they are for experts only.

Golf employs a similar system. Different colored tee markers represent various degrees of course difficulty. The farther back a marker on the tee box, the longer the hole plays; consequently, the harder it is.

Golfers should be realistic and not bite off more than they can chew. Play from the tees best suited to your skills. Red commonly designates ladies' tees, whites are for average players, blues for advanced players. On newer courses, there may be as many as five different tee markers, ranging from beginner to expert.

It is not at all unusual to have golfers play together from separate tees. One of golf's advantages is that it can be enjoyed by friends who share a passion for the game, if not the same ability.

On the first tee, each golfer makes an individual determination for the round: usually either red, white, or blue. As is true on the slopes, some decisions are better than others. The beginning skier who blithely defies the black diamond signs is in for an uncomfortable ride, literally learning his or her lesson by the seat of the pants.

Golfers can have equally momentous lapses of judgment. While no broken limbs are at stake, the price the golfer pays for choosing the wrong tee is time: time lost to him- or herself, to the foursome, and to all the golfers who follow.

Playing from the blues, or championship tees, when common sense dictates the more prudent selection of the whites, is not illegal. The green fee is the same for both. The rules are silent

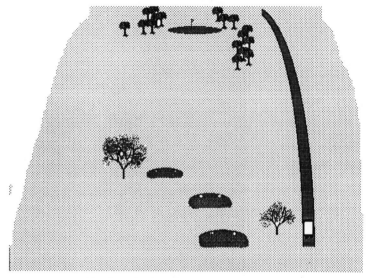

Play from the tee best suited to your skill level.

on the matter. But clearly, playing from the longer and more difficult back tees is often inappropriate and impetuous. Fortunately, the mistake can be quickly corrected on the next tee.

YOUR HONOR

Tradition bestows the *honor* of teeing off first to the player who won the previous hole, that is, played it in the lowest number of strokes. On the first tee, however, the honor must be determined some other way. Golfers often circle up and toss a tee into the air. Whomever it points to is accorded the honor for the first hole only. The procedure is repeated until the teeing order is determined. A popular method to pick teams is to throw three balls into the air. The owners of the balls that land closest to each other are partners. Another way to choose up sides is by handicap—pairing the highest and lowest together, for example. (The player with the honor on the first hole retains it until his or her score is bettered. From then on, whoever wins the hole has the honor.)

When slow play lurks, recreational golfers often forego the honor system and play *ready golf*. With ready golf, the player who reaches the tee and is ready to play first does so, regardless of who won the last hole. Dispensing with the formalities saves time otherwise spent waiting for everyone to gather and determine the honor. Ready golf also has a positive effect, speeding up those moving in the slow lane.

The honor system and ready golf can be joined. For a winning score, the honor may be duly awarded. But when the scores and play are undistinguished, it's first come, first served, ready golf. We recommend it. On the first tee, or if your group starts to fall behind, in the interests of time simply suggest it to your group.

X MARKS YOUR BALL

Gathering on the tee, golfers should announce their balls' brand and number. For additional identification purposes, each ball should be indelibly marked with a dot or an initial. Knowing your ball will save time when it gets confused with other balls on the course, as invariably happens.

YOU MAY FIRE WHEN READY

The group teeing off before yours should be well on their way by the time you reach the tee. Courtesy insists, however, that no one tee off until they are far enough out in the fairway. How far is far enough? The responsibility rests with the players on the tee. There are no hard and fast rules. Generally, if everyone in the preceding group has hit their second shots, it should be safe to play. That's . . . *should be*. It depends to a large extent on whether the group ahead is a foursome of rabbits or a foursome of tortoises. It will also depend on the group in front of *them*—and the group in front of *them*—and so on. If you have any doubts err on the side of caution. Wait until you're certain no one will get hit.

When the group ahead is out of range of some but not all players, the *shorter* hitters should go ahead and tee off. Never mind the honors. This helps keep play moving. In a tournament, however, doing so is against the rules. The honor must be maintained.

The first offense of hitting into a group, with suitable apologies, will probably be forgotten. The second offense will not. Don't let it happen a second time.

FIRST TEE JITTERS

Bernard Darwin, one of golf's finest writers, once noted that the first tee shot at the Old Course at St. Andrews, Scotland, was the easiest shot in golf. Strictly speaking, he was referring to the open fairway. But as every golfer who makes the pilgrimage knows, the first shot at the Old Course is anything but easy. With the august clubhouse of the Royal and Ancient Golf Club in the background and an assortment of locals gathered nearby, the mind wanders and the goosebumps and butterflies rise and flutter at will.

Every golfer struggles through a similar initiation every time the ball is on the tee. For some people, public speaking produces the same kind of discomfort. "Fear," wrote Tommy Armour, "ruins more golf shots, for duffer or star, than any other one factor." Bobby Jones blamed tension. This is probably not news to you, whatever you call it. Golfers instinctively take a practice swing or two to relax and cue their memory of a good swing.

This is perfectly acceptable. Problems arise, however, when one or two practice swings become three and four.

PRACTICE SWINGS

Practice swings were once actually illegal everywhere but on the tee. There are no posted legal limits about practice swings on the course today, but every golfer should recognize them for what they are: an agonizing source of slow play.

With adequate room on the tee there is no reason why golfers cannot take their practice swings at the same time, just as tennis players practice their serves together. The only time a practice swing should not be taken is when someone is preparing to swing in earnest.

One should suffice, two at the most. Remember, the golf course is not the place to experiment with your swing. It's not the place to learn a swing. The golf course is the place to play.

Longtime University of Texas football coach Darryl Royal used to say, "You've got to dance with the gal that brung ya." The same is true on the golf course. For better or worse, you've got to play with the swing you came with. Tinkering is for the range or lessons—on your own time.

Practice swings should be taken quickly, as much for practical reasons as common courtesy. The longer you stand over your ball, the tighter you get and the more fiendish tricks the mind plays. "Golf is not a chess match," Grantland Rice observed seventy years ago. "The longer you wait, the less chance you have to maintain the ease and rhythm of your stroke." The old adage "miss 'em quick" has a lot of merit. Consider Bobby Jones. From the start of his address to the moment his club struck the ball at impact, he was said to take all of three seconds. That's it. Some pros don't even take a practice swing. Players are often impervious to the negative effects of taking too many. Of course, there are others who, like rude drivers, couldn't care less. If you do take more than one practice swing, try to make up the time. Hustle to your ball or make an extra effort to help someone find theirs.

Throughout the course, but especially on the tee, maintain a conscious awareness of time. If you don't, the course officials and other golfers behind you will.

Slow play has little to do with how well you play. It afflicts duffers and professionals equally. Consider the comments of a promising young professional named Jack Nicklaus. He once told *Golf Digest*:

> My father had impressed me with the code of courtesy in golf, so I felt it was discourteous to a fellow player to be lining up a putt or otherwise preparing for the next shot while he was playing, because I might distract him. But Arnie, Joe Black and Jack Tuthill kept telling me to be ready when my turn came—without interfering with another player. That's a big part of the cure—to be ready.

Professionals are even fined for slow play. They have forty-five seconds to hit their shot from the time they reach their ball and the group in front is out of range. Playing in a timely manner is not rushing. It's having a sense of where you are, where you fit in on the course in relation to other golfers. As Jack says, it's also being ready to play when it's your turn.

STAND BY YOUR MAN

When a golfer steps between the markers and tees up his ball, the other golfers should stand together outside the markers, in view. Whenever possible, avoid standing directly behind a golfer preparing to play. This is true everywhere on the course, the equivalent in rudeness of looking over someone's shoulder when they're reading. When practice swings are being taken, conversation is OK. But when a player settles down to play, all conversation and movement should cease.

Wherever you stand, strive to be as unobtrusive as possible.

It doesn't take much to rattle a golfer. Jiggling coins, ripping open a glove, chatter—each is a discourteous distraction when someone is ready to play. This is especially true during a back-swing, when it tests the limits of human endurance. Until the swing is completed and the ball is on its way, stand still. If an inadvertent transgression is committed, offer an apology forthwith.

Some tee boxes are too small to allow for everyone to stand together. Wherever you stand, strive to be as unobtrusive as possible. (Incidentally, asking if you are in the way is a distraction in itself.)

HUMAN HAZARD #2

We've devoted a chapter to hazards. On the tee, however, you may encounter one of the human variety that bears brief discussion. Course regulars often take it upon themselves to provide newer players with impromptu guidance. It's one thing to point out the *makeup of a hole* to someone playing the course for the first time. It's something else to go out of one's way to alert the rookie to impending *trouble*, especially trouble that is clearly visible. (The scorecard or signs near the tee also provide hole descriptions.)

"Watch out for the pond on the right," however well intentioned, has the immediate effect of planting a most unwelcome seed and inducing one to hit—you guessed it—into the pond on the right. No good can come from this psychological warfare. Walter Hagen once completely unnerved an opponent by pointing out the rippling bicep muscles during his swing. The poor fellow was never the same, at least not until after the match.

In the course of your golfing career, you will see many unusual swings. You may admire them, marvel at them, or inwardly shake your head in dismay. But nothing is served by saying, "Your swing seems a little too *short* (or *long*, or *flat*, or *fast*, or *slow*, etc.). These casual observations seemingly tossed out of left field can be as destructive as a tornado. Your only defense against this line of attack (and similar broadsides) is a firm resolve and a healthy dose of tact.

After their shot, some players vacate the tee only grudgingly. Their ball may have stopped, but their own special brand of commentary is still rolling strong. Meanwhile, everyone waits patiently for an opening, as if it would be rude to do otherwise.

Don't wait for one. As soon as the previous shot is played, if you're ready, step up and tee up your ball. This sends an unmistakable signal to the slower player—next up. When the tee box is free, if no one steps forward, don't be shy. Golfers unfamiliar with the Rules of Etiquette often have an exaggerated sense of politeness. They'd rather wait for somebody to make the first move or be prompted to play than risk doing something wrong. It makes for a lot of unnecessary standing around. Remember, be ready to play. Have a tee and a ball in your hand.

ANYBODY SEE IT?

One sure way of making a friend out of a stranger during a round of golf is to make a conscious effort to help him or her find their ball. Especially on the tee, keep an eye out. It is often hard to follow the ball, especially your own.

When a ball is headed for the *rough*, try to find an object to line it up with for perspective—a tree, a house, whatever; anything to make the search easier. Of course, you've got enough to think about in finding your own ball. But a little consideration is easy, much appreciated, and will save time. You're all in this together, after all. On the next hole, you might need the help. Nothing can be more frustrating than splitting the fairway and not being able to find your ball.

MR. MULLIGAN

After a flubbed tee shot, many golfers feel it is their birthright to hit a *Mulligan*, a second shot. Not so. Many courses now make a point of prohibiting 'Mullys' under threat of expulsion—for good reason. They are an indefensible contributor to slow play.

Named for whomever (one theory cites a habitually late Canadian hotel worker), a Mulligan is a shot that doesn't exist in golf: a freebie, akin to First Ball In in tennis. It's a do-over, pretending the first flub never happened. Will the golfer who has never taken a Mulligan please step forward? Your Courtesy on the Course Award for Meritorious Service to Golf awaits. So will we, probably forever. Every golfer has taken one at some point.

Mulligans are naturally outlawed in tournaments. If you are invited to take a Mully, do it on the first tee—and only on the first tee. No more. And be quick about it. One per customer.

The exception is the social golf event circuit, where Mulligans are commonly sold to raise additional funds for charity. The limit is usually two per customer. They can be used anywhere on the course, which opens up a whole new decision—opening a can of worms that we'd rather not get into.

During recreational play, some golfers treat Mulligans like

beloved outlaws, looking the other way. Others are hopelessly addicted, with no hesitation about taking them at will anywhere on the course. This is a flat-out waste of time and can even be dangerous. To make your game more self-reliant, we recommend bucking up and going cold turkey.

You may, of course, hit a provisional. If you think your ball may be lost or out-of-bounds, wait until everyone has played, then announce your intention. Remember, you will be playing your fourth stroke from the fairway.

THROW THE CLUB HEAD

Tommy Bolt, a pro who had a reputation in such matters, once offered this advice to the budding club thrower: "If you are going to throw a club, it is important to throw it ahead of you, down the fairway, so you don't waste energy going back to pick it up." We have some additional thoughts. Don't throw the club. Put it back in your bag. Find your ball and hit it again.

Every golfer suffers golf's slings and arrows. Some do it with grace, some do it disgracefully. The former are a lot more fun to play with. Golf's torment is rooted in its inherent differences from other sports. The hallmarks of athleticism—strength, speed, instinct, and reflex—are ingredients for success in many sports. They also provide great ways for blowing off steam. Golf, however, relies less on brute strength, snap judgments, or instinctive reflexes. It affords plenty of time—too much of it—for reflection.

Rarely out of breath, golfers have ample opportunities to complain, bemoan, blame, carp, and crow. There isn't even a pitcher, a goalie, or anyone else to point the finger at. The ball is inert until you hit it. The course is right out in the open.

In every round there are two scores—the real score and the fantasy score. The fantasy score is the would've, could've, should've score. On the course, take care of the real score. War stories can wait for the 19th hole, to discuss over drinks after the round (when, again, your scorecard will come in handy).

Golfers are particularly creative with excuses. It's all that time they have. The wind, the lack of wind, the sun, the clouds, contact lenses, glasses—you name it, a golfer has found a way to work it into an alibi. And what's more, they believe it. "Complaints of one's own bad luck are in infinitely bad taste," Horace Hutchinson wrote in 1890. They still are. Golf has a phrase for tough luck. It's called the *rub of the green.*

In the beginning of the chapter, we noted that the first tee sets the pace for the round. It also sets the mood. "When we take pleasure in the game only according to the scorecard," wrote the author in *Bobby Jones on Golf,* "a bad start is likely to put entirely away the possibility of an enjoyable afternoon. The real way to enjoy golf is to take pleasure not in the score, but in the execution of the strokes."

"When you have any bit of hard luck, don't keep talking about it for several holes afterwards," H. J. Whigham advised in 1910. "Play the game for the fun of the thing; take your defeats cheerfully and your victories with modesty."

At the other extreme, there is at least one other species of golfer that bears discussion on the question of temperament. We mean the golfer who, during a bad, good, or even great round, comes out with, "It really doesn't matter how I play. I don't care what happens. I'm just here to get some air and get out of the house." To that, we say, "Who are you kidding?" Golf may be many things at different times, not all of them to our liking, but it will always be absorbing. We would do well to remember that despite what has happened, we are only one shot away from redemption and at least a partial cleansing of the slate.

If these people do in fact believe that golf is (gasp!) only a game, they should keep their opinions to themselves and not spoil the fun for the rest of us.

Between the extremes of club throwing, on the one hand, and blasé indifference on the other, there is a middle ground. With your tee shot as well as your temperament, we hope you find the middle ground, more commonly known as the fairway.

CHAPTER FOUR CHECKLIST

___ Take inventory.
  ___Enough tees?   ___Balls?
  ___Divot repairer?   ___Ball marker?
  ___Scorecard?   ___Pencil?
___ Always carry an extra ball in your pocket.
___ Play from the tees best suited to your skills.
___ Having trouble keeping up? Suggest ready golf.
___ Identify your ball on the first tee.
___ Never tee off until the preceding group is safely away.
___ To save time, shorter hitters should tee off first.
___ Take practice swings at the same time, if feasible.
___ Practice swings or conversation are permissible until some-
      one addresses their ball.
___ Beware of the negative effects of taking too many practice
      swings.
___ Miss 'em quick.
___ Avoid standing directly behind someone preparing to play.
___ Hold still while others swing.
___ Never ask if you are in the way. You will be told if you are.
___ Be ready to play when it's your turn. Step up to the tee box.
___ Once you've played, vacate the tee box immediately.
___ Make a conscious effort to watch everyone's ball. Line it up
      with trees, rocks, etc.
___ Mulligans are an indefensible source of slow play.
___ Tinkering with your swing is for the range or lessons, on
      your own time.
___ "Complaints of one's own bad luck are in infinitely bad
      taste."

CHAPTER FOUR GLOSSARY

Dogleg—A hole where the fairway bends to the left or right.

Fat, Thin—Slang descriptions of mis-hits. A fat shot takes too much turf behind the ball. A thin shot catches the ball above the center of the club head.

Honor—By lot or virtue of the low score on the previous hole, the right to tee off or play first.

Makeup of a Hole—Elements or distinguishing features of a hole; hazards, for example.

Mulligan—The gratuitous replaying of a shot.

Ready Golf—Name given to attempt to save time by foregoing honor. The player ready to play first plays.

Rough—Area off the fairway, but not in a hazard, where grass is allowed to grow higher.

Short Hitter—Comparison description of player who doesn't hit the ball far.

Short, Long, Flat, Fast, Slow—Terms used to describe varying swings. Short and long speak to the length of the backswing; fast and slow to the speed of the swing. A flat swing moves horizontally rather than in an upright plane.

Tee Box—Starting place for each hole. The tee markers define the area from which the ball must be played.

Trouble—Slang for course pitfalls, including hazards, rough, etc.

ON THE FAIRWAY

PUTTING THE CART BEFORE THE COURSE

NO ONE YELLS "Start your engines!" after a foursome tees off, but on many courses it wouldn't sound absurd. A fivesome was spotted recently on a municipal course; it happened to be in Texas, but it could have been anywhere in the United States. Each golfer drove his own cart!

Perhaps our love affair with the automobile provides at least a partial answer for their popularity. The more pedestrian answer is simply profit. Whatever the reason, carts are a part of the game. Even the most devout walker will ride occasionally.

Golf carts, or, as they used to be called, golf cars, more closely resemble their frivolous cousin, the go-cart. Although far sturdier, golf carts have been known to roll over cliffs, fall into lakes, or even flip over. A gasoline-powered cart weighs about 900 pounds; battery-operated carts are even heavier. Even without two adult passengers and two sets of clubs, that's a lot of weight to be rolling around the fragile environment of a course. And while they'd never be mistaken for a Ferrari, a cart can attain speeds of up to 15 miles per hour. That's fast enough. Carelessness in any form—quick accelerations, sharp turns, or screeching halts—are at best inconsiderate and rude as well as detrimental to course conditions; at worst, they're dangerous.

Always start slowly, making sure your partner is seated before you drive off. Set the brake firmly when you stop. On steep downhills pump the brake gently before stopping, as you would driving a car. If you don't feel comfortable behind the wheel, let someone else handle the driving.

Extra yards and the occasional spectacular bounce aside, cart paths provide a road that in turn protects the course from cart traffic. On many courses, especially at more exclusive clubs and resorts, carts are relegated exclusively to the path. This restriction may also apply any time the course is wet or particularly sensitive.

THE 90 DEGREE RULE

There are three rules regarding cart operation on the course: Unrestricted, Cart Paths Only, and the 90 Degree Rule. When carts are allowed to roam, follow the signs and common sense. Keep carts on the path as often as possible and never drive on the *fringe* or the green. Unrestricted does not mean anything goes.

Cart Paths Only means just that: carts must stay exclusively on the path. Perhaps the only exception would be to pull over just enough to let another vehicle pass. (Access may also be extended to handicapped golfers.)

To save time when this rule is in effect, pull the cart farther up the path, halfway between two balls separated in the fairway. Doing so helps the flow of the game. Golfers won't have to take two steps back (to retrieve the cart) to take two steps forward.

The *90 Degree Rule* prevents golfers from riding to their balls as the crow flies. The cart is allowed to move only on a 90 degree angle (hence the name) across the fairway to the ball, then straight back again to the path before proceeding.

Another timesaver is club selection. When carts are not allowed in the fairway, if you can't anticipate which club to use

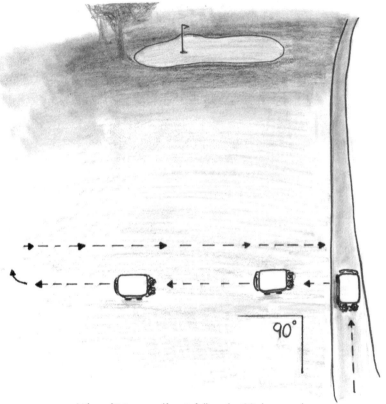

When driving a golf cart, follow the 90 degree rule.

(from the cart path), take several. The cart path might also help you decide. Yardage markers are often placed nearby or painted on it. The key to the markings—for example, yellow markers equal 200 yards, blue markers equal 150 yards—is on the score-card. As you ride, keep an eye out for markers and other distance landmarks also noted on the card.

THE LAY OF THE LAND

Carts do cover ground faster, which has its advantages. On blind spots, a cart affords the opportunity of driving ahead to quickly survey the lay of the land. A little reconnaissance might also prevent playing into the group ahead. Doing so, however, should be done only in moderation and for good reason, never when it slows play.

Any time the cart is off the path, be aware of wet or soft areas, even on sunny days. The damage caused by riding through puddles can take weeks to repair.

A LITTLE FORETHOUGHT

The Cart Paths Only rule is in effect. Your ball lies on the opposite side of the fairway from the cart path and your partner's ball. Do you

a) Select the club you think you'll need, hit the ball, then return to the cart?
b) Grab several clubs—both for this shot and the next one; then, after you play, walk ahead to your ball, leaving the cart to your partner?
c) Take one club, walk to your ball, change your mind, then yell to your partner to throw you the proper club?

Ideally, (b) is the best answer. Thinking ahead, select the clubs you anticipate needing for this—and for the next—shot. How can you know which club you'll need before you reach your ball? Often, you can't. The best thing to do is to give yourself a choice. Taking several clubs will save you countless trips back to the cart.

Here's another situation: The 90 Degree Rule is in effect. Your ball is on the far side of the fairway. Your partner's ball is nearer the cart path. Do you

Keep the cart even with—not in front of,
not behind—the person playing.

a) Park the cart by your partner's ball, wait for him or her to play, then drive together to your ball?

b) Leave the cart on the path, wait until your partner plays, then walk to your ball?

c) Drop off your partner with several clubs, and take the cart to your ball?

Correct answer: (c)

WARNING: Anytime you take several clubs out onto the fairway, the risk of losing them increases. To prevent misfortune, always place the clubs even with or a little in front and to the side of your ball, never behind you. Keeping them in sight makes them harder to forget.

PARALLEL PARKING

Since it is impolite to stand behind a golfer, it follows that the same is true with a half-ton vehicle. Never pull the cart up onto someone's heels or anywhere remotely near enough to be in the way. You could run over a ball or a club, not to mention a foot. Park even with the golfer but far enough aside so as not to be a distraction, just as you stand on the tee. Lagging back within someone's peripheral vision is distracting. Keep up even; not in front of the golfer, not behind.

BACKBRAKING

Sitting behind the wheel waiting for your partner to play a shot, mind your feet. Unconscious playing with the pedals could result in defiance of one of golf's commandments: Thou Shalt Not Release the Cart Brake During a Backswing.

Less obvious and only slightly less provocative is the sound of clubs carelessly returned to their bag. You are asked to find less conspicuous and noisy ways to vent your frustration.

BABY-SITTING

With small children along as passengers in your cart, courtesy insists they be kept at a safe distance during your partners' shots. A safe distance is defined as well enough out of earshot and far enough out of sight so that sudden bursts of sound or movement will not cause a distraction.

HOOFING IT

Getting your money's worth is one thing. Because you paid to rent a cart does not mean you can't occasionally leave it behind and walk to your ball. Don't wait for ball-to-ball service. It will often be faster if you grab a club, hop out, and let your partner drive off with the cart to his or her shot. Whenever it is appropriate, i.e., in the interests of time, hoof it.

Ropes and signs will indicate the cart path.

Observe the on-course markers as you would traffic signals, which is what they are. The green will often be roped off, or signs will advise you where to return the cart to the path. The ropes are there solely to prevent carts from providing limo service up to or, we shudder to think, actually onto the green. If, however, the ropes impede your stance or swing, feel free to remove them temporarily. After you play just make sure they are replaced.

THE CLUB CARRIER

We'll leave the subject of vehicles behind for the moment. A quick word on their more humble forebear: the pull cart. You should know that if your pull cart experience does not include your bag toppling forward on occasion, clubs akimbo, consider yourself lucky. They can be as responsive as old shopping carts and just as squeaky.

Pull carts, like riding carts, should never traverse a green. Their operators should maintain a similar vigilance to avoid leaving tire tracks on fairway soft spots. The electric pull cart has proved a popular alternative to riding. Their high-tech metabolism ensures substantial rental fees while their comparatively light weight protects courses from the ravages of the horseless carriage.

Some golfers make the casual mistake of leaving their pull carts a few feet behind each time they approach their ball. To swing often requires a quick backtrack to push the cart out of the way. It also means they have to walk back to walk forward. Better still, as with riding carts, pull the cart up even and to the side. To retrieve it, or change clubs, then requires only a step.

TURN, TURN, TURN

Golf is structured in such a way as to remove the guesswork about turn taking. You are expected to know your spot in the order. No one should have to be prodded or even prompted.

With everyone spread out on the fairway, it's imperative that golfers act decisively and adhere to established protocol: first, to keep play moving; second, so no one gets beaned; third, to honor tradition. Many golfers are, again, needlessly timid and over-cautious. A stalemate of sorts results that slows play and fuels their own discomfort.

The timid hesitate when they should swing. Too far apart to converse, a gesture coyly implies, "You first." Across the fairway, eyes respond as if to say, "No, I couldn't. After you." Then the wordless reply, "I insist." And so on, and so on. If someone says to you, "Go ahead," or simply pauses to look at you, do the right thing. Hit the ball. Playing quickly does not mean playing carelessly. It means being ready to play, then playing.

The timid hesitate when they should swing.

There is no penalty for hitting out of turn. If you have any doubt, so long as the coast is clear, go ahead and swing. Some may do it in fewer strokes than others, but golf is one sport in which no one is denied a turn. It's often said that golf is the only game in which the object is to play less of it.

The first person to play is the person whose ball lies farthest from the green. This is known as being *away,* or out. The order continues until everyone reaches the green. (If you are playing ready golf, the first person ready to play, plays.)

While this first person is walking to their ball, selecting a club, checking distance, testing the wind, adjusting their cap, or otherwise preparing to play, others should find their balls. When the address begins in earnest, that's the signal to stand still, if you are nearby. The player who continues to creep forward ever so slowly during someone's swing will justly find this disrespect rewarded with an icy stare.

A rhythm should become evident as the round progresses, and in no sport is rhythm so important to success as it is in golf. Move to the ball, hit it, keep moving. There should be as little standing around as possible. You are required to be quiet and motionless only while others are actually addressing and hitting their balls.

Use the time walking to locate distance markers, taking note of other features of the hole you will have to consider. Yardage is often posted on the tops of sprinkler heads on the ground or is denoted by colored stakes or the position of certain trees along the fairway. Consult the scorecard.

Yardage is routinely calculated to the middle of the green. Of course, the hole may be set anywhere on the green—back, middle, or front. The color of the flag may tip you off to the *pin placement* (the location of the flag on the green), a difference potentially as great as twenty-five or thirty yards. A common three-color system might use white flags to clue golfers to pins placed (or "cut") in the front of the green; blue flags to reflect holes positioned in the center of the green; and yellow flags to guide golfers to shoot for the back of the green. Smaller flags, or plastic balls, attached to the flagstick may also indicate the location of the hole. If the ball is set higher on the flag, it may mean the hole is in the back.

HUMAN HAZARD #3

The important question of yardage will prove irresistible to our friend, the human hazard. The person who was kind enough to remind you on the tee about the hazard you were doing your best to ignore will be certain to follow up. As you choose your club and prepare to swing, the innocent question "Are you sure you've got *enough club*?" is the fairway equivalent of "Make sure you avoid the out-of-bounds on the right." It serves the same demonic purpose. Since it is your shot, your swing, your ball, and your score, you must make an executive decision and savor the glory or suffer the consequences. Again, a stiff upper lip is advised. No matter how brazen the remark, no verbal response is required, or recommended, to questions of this nature.

However well intentioned, our friend the HH (who may be more than just a friend) may go one step further, offering not only advice, but instruction. Spouses, parents, friends and lovers are particularly susceptible to this vice. For the record, on-course instruction by someone other than a qualified professional wastes time, is a distraction to other players, and rarely has a positive effect. We strongly recommend against it. A milder form, known as *clubbing* (suggesting what club another golfer should use), by anyone other than their caddy is equally bad form. Prolonged exposure may result in a golfer invoking a different and more literal interpretation to "clubbing."

As you prepare to swing, you will feel all eyes upon you. This can be daunting in any situation, especially an endeavor as vexing as golf. You should realize, however, that the reasons golfers scrutinize each other are entirely logical. Of course, deep down they may harbor a fiendish interest in your misfortune or a suspicion of foul play, but the real reasons golfers watch each other are simply to avoid being hit and so they will not miss their own cue to play. It's nothing personal. It's simply to keep the game moving.

PRACTICE SWINGS (AGAIN)

Take as many practice swings as you want. Honest. When players are still on the green ahead of you, or there is some other delay, help yourself. Practice swings are only a nuisance when they contribute to slow play. And nowhere is it written that practice swings can't be taken as judiciously after a shot as before it. Take half a dozen, if you want, so long as it doesn't slow your group down. When the way in front is clear, then the meter is running. One practice swing is then the considerate number to take.

CAN I PLAY?

In the fairway, as on the tee, you will have to decide when it is safe to play. With respect to the group ahead, if there is a 1 in 100 chance of hitting the perfect shot—say, reaching the green while others are on it—hold off. Use the distance markers to help you decide.

It is small consolation to learn that you have been hit by accident. If such a mistake occurs (once is a mistake, twice is a provocation), the plaintive cry of *"FORE!"* should be shouted. It warns all within range to take cover. On any errant shot, yours or someone else's, sound the alarm.

Your perfect shot may not even hit someone. After all, a ball rolling onto a green poses no danger to those standing on it. Nevertheless, it is an inexcusable breach of manners and should be treated as such. It may not physically hurt anyone, but it will play havoc with their concentration.

There is no excuse for hitting into another group. No salvos fired across the bow are permissible, no wake-up calls allowed to get a slower group to pick up the pace. There are more civil and effective methods. We'll get to them in a moment. We do acknowledge that mistakes can happen, even when we are being careful. Even the great Jones once underestimated his ability and hit into a group during casual play. He spent the rest of the round apologizing. That may have been overdoing it, but anytime "FORE!" is heard, a sincere apology should not be far behind.

Courtesy on the course is not something offered only to your foursome. It starts there and extends to every golfer on the course.

Duffer or champion, it makes no difference. Everyone should be treated civilly.

D IS FOR DIVOT

Many varied Rules there are
On which our golf game pivots,
But one stands out, beyond a doubt,
"Please replace the divots."

—From "Noteworthy," by W. Hastings Webling, 1920

Nothing so easily prevented is more debilitating to course conditions over time than neglected divots. A bucket of sand and a small shovel are often provided on the back of many carts. The idea is that you will use these tools to fill the marks caused by swinging a club.

Replacing divots is the cornerstone of proper etiquette. There's nothing more discouraging than finding a great shot nestled inside a divot. Like litter, they have an insidious, cumulative effect on morale. When a course looks pillaged rather than played, not only does the course suffer, but so do the golfers. The game is above all an opportunity to get out and enjoy the outdoors. When the course is thoughtlessly scarred, the whole experience is cheapened.

Simply take the errant turf and press it back into place. As you go, if you spot and replace a divot other than your own, well done. Even if it won't help the grass grow back faster, replacing divots improves the course appearance.

PLAYING THROUGH

Nothing requires more diplomacy on the golf course than playing through. Many golfers would sooner negotiate with terrorists than yield their right-of-way to an intimidating, albeit faster, playing group. What should be a smooth transition can with a little snobbery come off as an affront. Newer golfers are often left with an undeniable whiff of inferiority. What they forget is that golf is not a race. Giving way to faster players is not an admission of defeat. It is the right thing to do.

Not to be outdone are the play-throughers—rather than the play-throughees—who view the opportunity to pass as a special gift. They are mistaken. Playing through is not a birthright. It is, rather, a courtesy; as such, it must be offered to be accepted. Better players cannot assume the privilege if the group ahead is keeping pace with the group ahead of it. Don't confuse speed of play with ability. Many better players play as slow as molasses and are justly taken to task for it.

The foursome is golf's standard unit of measure. Four hours is the approximate time it should take a foursome to play eighteen holes. Foursomes playing in a timely manner are under no obligation to allow smaller groups to play through. When the course is crowded, twosomes that encounter other twosomes or singles should pair up.

Common sense dictates the rules on playing through. If there is a hole open in front of your group (no one on the tee box, fairway, or green of the next hole), then a waiting group should be invited to play through. A lost ball and the subsequent search for it (five minutes tops) is reason enough to wave a group on. Move carts, bags, and bodies out of the way. Be as unobtrusive as possible. Don't present a target.

It must be one of Murphy's, or somebody else's, Laws, but when a group is playing through, their play invariably takes a sudden disastrous turn. Perhaps it's the additional pressure of having seven pairs of eyes watching instead of just three. Who can say? At any rate, when this happens, buck up and bear it bravely. Say nothing. Let them through.

When the course is not crowded, it is customary to let smaller groups pass. Two usually play faster than four. The mistake most often made is when golfers inexplicably refuse to let anyone pass, come hell or high water. To avoid this and other unpleasant situations, courses are routinely patrolled by marshals, course officials who try to keep play moving. When one cannot be found, save your complaints for the pro shop. Do not raise the tension level by confronting the guilty party and airing it out. They will get the message eventually, one way or another.

A good place to play through is at the *turn,* after your group has completed the *front side,* or first nine holes. Instead of repairing to the clubhouse for a midround snack, ask politely if your group might keep going and begin the *back side,* or last nine holes. By the time the slower group returns from its pause for refreshment, you will be well on your way. No hard feelings.

The shorter par-3 holes are also convenient spots to play through or allow a group to pass. The slower group should play their tee shots, walk to the green, mark their balls, move off the green, then signal back to the tee to allow the faster group to proceed. The onus is then on the second group to play through without delay. No Mulligans. No stopping to scour for balls. A thank you is appropriate when the switch has been completed. (Reminder: Remember what ball you're playing. If you don't know which ball is yours, how will anyone else?)

The tee is the least disruptive place to give way. Everyone is together, in reasonable comfort, and play can be resumed without an unnatural pause. You can use the time productively to practice swings or trade notes or just enjoy the camaraderie and scenery. Whenever you let a group play through, be it on the fairway, the green, or especially on the tee, don't resume play until the faster group is safely out of range.

ANYBODY LOSE A WEDGE?

Any time you discover a discarded club or anything of value on the course (a head cover, a wallet, a glove, whatever), don't leave it there. Clubs especially should be carried along and delivered to the pro shop. Chances are someone will turn up looking for them a hole or two later.

Once a club is gone, unless you've marked it with a phone number or address, the odds of recovery diminish as time passes. Most often left behind are putters or wedges, clubs with sentimental attachment that make their loss a greater misfortune. There are locating services listed in the back of magazines that will search to find a match to help complete a set. If the club is of recent make, the manufacturer will be able to replace a lost club for you. Before you have to go through all that, if you have lost a club, check the lost-club bin, keep calling the pro shop, and post a note on available bulletin boards in the clubhouse.

FREEBIES

Searching for lost balls, you're as likely to find someone else's ball as your own. The temptation is often too great not to collect a stray ball in the rough, or even on the fairway. The ball may indeed be abandoned, in which case you are welcome to it. But before you risk petty larceny, you had better be darn sure it's lost. Balls routinely end up in the wrong fairway, sometimes by design. The owner may soon be close at hand, and you can bet his or her ball was not intended as a gift.

When you spy a ball that you know is not yours and other golfers are approaching, without lifting it, note the make and number. Being able to pass along the information that "there's a Silver King over by that elm" is a thoughtful and effortless courtesy that will save time. Of course, knowing your own ball's brand and number will make finding it easier.

TIME OUT

The snack cart is a welcome, if disruptive, influence during a round. At country clubs, a signature will pass for payment. On public courses, it's cash on the barrel head. Try to keep the delay to a minimum. If you are ready to hit your shot and the cart arrives, hit it and then proceed to your reward. If your wallet's handy, you might use the occasion to buy a round for your partners. Or just to save time, you might spring for it and settle up later. If you'd rather not interrupt your game, water is almost always provided at regular intervals. (Be careful leaving open sodas or beers in your cart. Bees love to climb inside.)

HUNTING FOR EASTER EGGS

Perhaps it's the Scottish reputation for thrift or the thrill of the hunt, like the excitement children experience searching for Easter eggs or presents. Whatever the reason, it is hard for some golfers to pass by a ball, there for the taking, even if it may lie at the bottom of a cliff or under three feet of murky water. At many courses, no sooner does a ball ripple into the woods than someone appears, like a troll from under a bridge, and begins beating the bushes with an old club or ball retriever.

Looking for lost balls is good sport and good fun. Problems arise, however, when it threatens to compete with play. It is not unusual to come upon two carts, seemingly abandoned in the middle of the fairway. Where are the occupants? In the vicinity searching for their own balls? No, they're trolling for others. If you can't resist the lure of hidden treasure, keep one eye peeled for oncoming traffic and wave the "golfers" through. Happy hunting as long as you don't inconvenience others. Remember, the real hunt (the one for better scores) lies ahead.

CHAPTER FIVE CHECKLIST

The Rules of the Road
___ Don't drive a cart if you're uncomfortable behind the wheel.
___ Quick accelerations, sharp turns, and screeching halts are at best inconsiderate, at worst dangerous.
___ Walk when you can, anticipate your next shot, and take a few clubs.
___ Watch out for and avoid all wet spots and ground under repair.
___ Never park behind a golfer. Stay even, preferably out of his peripheral vision.
___ Never release the brake during someone's swing. (?!#?!@!)
___ Know the difference between the 90 Degree Rule and Cart Paths Only.

On Foot
___ Pull handcarts even with your ball.
___ Play decisively. Don't wait to be told. No one should have to be prodded or even prompted to play.
___ One practice swing is enough when people are waiting.
___ Don't creep when others are hitting nearby.
___ Look for stakes or distance posted on sprinkler heads.
___ Don't slow down the game with preshot advice.
___ Shout "FORE!" when you hit a shot that may hit someone.
___ There are no excuses for hitting into the group ahead.
___ Replace your divots!—and others that you see.
___ Letting a group play through is the right thing to do. Don't resume play until they're out of range.
___ Five minutes searching for a lost ball—max!
___ Don't let hunting for Easter eggs become paramount.

CHAPTER FIVE GLOSSARY

Away—The ball farthest from the hole. When a golfer is away, it is his or her turn. Same as "out."

Bite—To land a ball with backspin on the green.

Enough Club—The appropriate club for a given yardage.

FORE!—Accepted warning when golfers are endangered.

90 Degree Rule—Cart restriction that allows carts to enter and exit fairways only on a 90 degree angle.

Pin Placement—The location of the hole (or pin) on the green. Regularly rotated.

Turn—The midway point between the first nine holes (front side) and the last nine holes (back side).

6
IN A HAZARD

A HAZARDOUS MIX OF DREAD AND DELIGHT

AS PATIENT AS sea anemones and only slightly less sinister, certain obstacles, appropriately called hazards, dot the course. They may be ancient hollows filled with sand, formed by sheep seeking shelter from the wind, as the first sand bunkers were at St. Andrews. They may be as graceful as gentle streams, as garish as artificial waterfalls, or as grand as the Pacific Ocean. Signatures of the architect, hazards are where they are and what they are on purpose, designed to instill both dread and delight. Man-made or appropriated from nature, their presence adds another layer of complexity to the game. Golf is more than mechanically mastering the swing. It requires strategy and tactics. The biggest obstacle hazards present is not physical but mental. Most of all, hazards make us think.

They issue an eternally tantalizing challenge: *lay up* (play safe), bypassing the danger; or "go for it" and court disaster attempting to *carry* (or clear) the hazard.

While we may curse them at times, hazards give a course character. Some even have names: Hell Bunker, the Coffins, Willie Campbell's Grave (he's not buried there—but apparently his game once was), Kruger and Mrs. Kruger, Sahara, and the Himalayas.

It is worth remembering that hazards make a course not only

difficult but more interesting and pleasing to the eye. By definition something to avoid, hazards are nevertheless part of the game, and as such they deserve the same consideration from players as the tee, the fairway, or the green.

Officially, there are three kinds of hazards: bunkers, water hazards, and lateral water hazards. Bunkers are easily recognized and more commonly known as sand traps (See Chapter 3).

STORMING THE BUNKER

Bunkers should always be entered and exited from the low side. Never storm the beach by leaping in from above or exit by

Proper way to enter and exit a bunker.

climbing out the top. The sides and the *lips* (rim) are especially fragile and easily damaged by carelessness. At the very least, jumping into a bunker worsens its complexion by removing sand from its sides.

DON'T FORGET TO RAKE

Before you enter a bunker, first find the rake and place it nearby. You are obligated to provide a little interim maintenance, raking your footprints and marks after you play in consideration of the next victim. A ball that lands in a footprint is as unpleasant as finding a shot nestled in a fairway divot. When you have played your ball free, retrace your steps, raking backward. Leave the rake outside the bunker on either side, face down and out of the way. Don't chuck it. Extra clubs (putter, wedge) should be left outside the bunker.

Always rake the bunker after you have played out of it.

If your ball comes to rest against the rake, as sometimes happens, simply remove the rake and play the ball where it lies. There is no penalty if the ball moves.

GROUNDED

One absolute in all hazards: you may not ground your club (Penalty: two strokes). The club head may not touch the ground, the sand, or the water until you actually swing. You may not use your club as a cane. You may not test the bunker's consistency with your club.

Why not? It's against the rules, for one, but common sense applies, the same common sense behind replacing divots and ball marks: to preserve the course. Imagine what a sand bunker would look like if every golfer who hit into one was first allowed a few healthy swipes? There would soon be nothing left.

PREPARE FOR LIFT-OFF

Uncertainty is a hazard's biggest obstacle. For various reasons, such as not being able to take a dry run with a real practice swing, it's impossible to know precisely what will happen. The possibilities are infinite. Varieties of sand differ from one region to the next. Changing weather conditions may alter the shot. The sand may be dry and fluffy or wet and hard. It may be soft on top, firm underneath. The ball may lie on the surface or be almost completely buried.

Since no one is positive of the result, it is imperative that the person playing be given a wide berth. The ball might float to earth like a parachute or come out faster than a speeding bullet.

When someone is playing from a bunker, especially to the green, stand aside. Do not linger near the flag or line up your

Head's Up!

putt. It's terribly distracting to have to worry about where everyone is in addition to playing a tough shot. Until it has been played, as much for your own safety, courtesy insists that you keep your distance. Get to a safe position and stand still. When you are ready to play your shot, "heads up" might be in order to provide some advance warning.

LOOSE IMPEDIMENTS, ETC.

One other essential hazard rule: you may not lift or touch loose impediments. If twigs, grass clippings, leaves, or other natural objects have found their way into the bunker, there they must remain. They cannot be removed. You may lift obstructions, man-made objects such as cans, bottles, clubs, or the rake, if left inside the hazard.

It is not uncommon to find your ball partially submerged in a pool of collected rainwater at the bottom of a sand bunker in need of repair. Under these circumstances, you may move the ball, without penalty, to another part of the bunker that is dry and play from there. You are not allowed to move your ball out of the hazard or drop it closer to the hole.

IS THAT ME?

When more than one player hits into the same bunker, some confusion is understandable. With balls partially buried, it's entirely possible that a case of mistaken identity can result in a wrong ball being played.

Don't worry. There's no penalty for playing a wrong ball out of a hazard, but do not pick up the ball to identify it. Swing away. If a mistake occurs, the owner whose ball has been accidentally played should drop a new ball on the same spot (after the bunker has been raked and returned to its original condition) and play on from there. The original lie should be similarly recreated. If the ball was completely buried to begin with— before the mistake occurred—that's how it should be again.

AWAY

The player who is in a bunker cannot necessarily assume he or she has the right-of-way. It depends, as it does everywhere else on the course, on who is farthest from the hole. That person has the honor, be it from the fairway, the bunker, or the green.

CLUB SAND WEDGE

The sand wedge is designed specifically to extricate a ball from sand, although it is also useful to pitch with from short distances. Unlike a 9-iron or a pitching wedge, it is more lofted and has a larger *flange*. These features make it easier to bounce off sand. Better ranges offer practice bunkers to work on your sand play. Playing late in the afternoon during the week also offers opportunities to hone your skills. Just don't forget to rake.

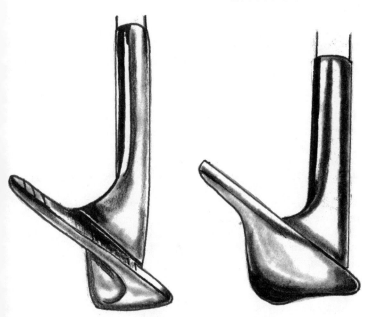

Pitching wedge vs. sand wedge.

THE HAND MASHIE

When things go wrong, another serviceable way of getting out of the cat box, the beach, the sandbox, or the dozen or so other terms used to describe sand bunkers is the hand mashie. In tournament play, unless you declare an *unplayable lie,* you are obligated to whack away as many times as it takes until either you, the sand, or daylight gives out and play is postponed.

In recreational play, however, after three or four unsuccessful tries (each made quickly and decisively—in the interests of time and sanity), throw the ball out of the bunker or pick up. Let the game proceed. Embarrassing? Yes, but doing so will be a lot more welcome than stubbornness and delay. You'll have ample opportunities to redeem yourself.

WATER

Water hazards are defined by yellow stakes or lines and usually include some dry ground around the water. Recreational players commonly carry "water balls," stand-ins for a new ball. It is permissible to substitute a stunt double, with one proviso. The water ball must never be one "borrowed" from the driving range.

You are welcome to play a ball out of shallow water or out of any hazard. Just remember that the club cannot touch the water (that would be grounding) until the actual stroke begins. A water hazard does not have to be filled with water. It can be a drainage ditch or a dried creek bed. Look for the stakes or lines for guidance.

DROP AREA

A local ruling will sometimes provide for a *drop area,* designated with a circle or a sign. It's often used as a way of speeding up play on holes where hitting over water is involved. After one or two shots go into the water (depending upon the rule), instead of trying again ad infinitum, golfers are permitted to take a drop, bypass the hazard and play on for the cost of one stroke.

> Situation: If a player must move to the drop area after hitting his tee shot into the water, what number shot will be played from the drop area?
>
> Answer: 3. One for the first shot that goes into the water, two for the penalty, three for the next shot from the drop area.

In formal competition, none of this exists. As with sand bunkers, there are no limits, no relief, no maximum number of strokes before a new pitcher comes in or a player fouls out. There is a lot of humor in hazards even if they do require, like a frightful vacation, the passing of time before the pathos can be fully appreciated.

HOW TO CORRECTLY TAKE A DROP

Stand erect, hold the ball at shoulder height and arm's length, and drop it. If it rolls into the hazard twice (or rolls toward the hole or more than two club lengths), you are permitted to place the ball on the ground—not anywhere you want, however. It must be put as near as possible to the spot where the ball hit the ground when you dropped it.

Taking a drop.

LATERAL

A lateral water hazard is distinguished by red lines or red stakes. The key difference between it and other hazards is location. As the name implies, a lateral hazard is usually parallel to the fairway.

For the cost of one stroke, you are allowed to drop your ball two club lengths from the boundary of the hazard, at the spot where the ball entered the hazard. You can use any club in your bag to measure the two club lengths. Most golfers use the longest club, the driver. Whichever club you use, you must not advance your ball closer to the hole.

NOW WHAT?

During a match, confusion over the rules can be cleared up by consulting the Rule Book, tournament officials, or your playing partners. If there is still no consensus, play two balls. Play the first from the spot you think is correct, the other from the position someone else believes is proper. Finish the hole with each ball, recording two scores. Consult the pro when you reach the clubhouse. Your score for the hole, and final score, should be determined according to his decision.

In a famous incident at the 1958 Masters, Arnold Palmer discovered his ball badly embedded behind the 12th hole. After he scored a 5 with the original ball, Arnie insisted he be allowed to play a second ball, invoking a local embedded-ball rule then in effect. He took the free drop and scored a 3 with the second ball. The second score counted, and it provided his eventual margin of victory: one stroke.

HUMAN HAZARD #4

When someone's ball *finds* (or lands in) a hazard, there is no need to comment on the injustice of it all, no need to crowd around dwelling at length over the impossibility of the next shot. Your time will come. Indifference is best.

Treat whatever happens with the sobriety of an English butler. Making light of our own mishaps is one thing, displaying obvious enjoyment over another's is something else. No matter how comical or disastrous the results, remember: "In misfortune, even to smile is to offend."

Hazards can bring out the worst in temperament. Harping on our bad luck gets old very quickly. In other circumstances, the jury would probably find unanimously (and in record time) that bad luck had not occurred, but that a bad shot had. The longer we dwell on our mistakes, of course, the more debilitating they become to our golf. When someone gets into trouble, nothing needs to be said.

"If your adversary is badly bunkered," advised Horace Hutchinson, "there is no rule against your standing over him and counting his strokes aloud, with increasing gusto as their number mounts up; but it will be a wise precaution to arm yourself with the niblick before doing so, so as to meet him on equal terms."

CHAPTER SIX CHECKLIST

___ When someone gets into trouble, nothing needs to be said.
___ Bunkers should always be entered and exited from the low side.
___ Don't touch your (or anyone else's) ball to identify it.
___ Never ground your club in a hazard.
___ In casual play, toss your ball out after three or four unsuccessful attempts.
___ Always rake bunkers. When you're finished, leave the rake outside the bunker on either side, facedown.

___ "Water" balls are permissible only in recreational play.
___ Know how to take a drop correctly.
___ Rules dispute? Play two balls, then consult the pro.
___ Red lines or stakes—lateral water hazard.
___ Yellow lines or stakes—water hazard. Know the difference.

CHAPTER SIX GLOSSARY

Carry—To successfully clear a hazard.

Drop Area—Designated area where balls are dropped and played.

Finds—Slang for where the ball lands. A ball that finds the hazard has landed in the hazard.

Flange—Iron club head feature that flares out. Usually noted in reference to sand or pitching wedges.

Lay Up—Short but safe play.

Unplayable Lie—A ball in a position that cannot be played; a determination made by the player.

ON THE GREEN

WALTZ SOFTLY ON GOLF'S DANCE FLOOR

IT'S BEEN SAID that driving is an art, iron play a science, and putting an inspiration. Putting continues to confound generations of golfers to the brink of madness. The sad fact of it is the longer and the better one plays, the more maddening putting becomes. Nothing in golf is more admired when done well or vilified when done poorly. Nothing that seems such child's play one moment can be so incomprehensible the next.

Once nicknamed the "dance floor," the putting green is the one place on the course where courtesy can be literally trampled underfoot. With everyone reunited in a relatively confined area, mistakes are magnified. A little fancy footwork may at times be required. But more often than not, as on the rest of the course, the most common mistake is timidity and indecision.

The putting green should always be treated with a degree of reverence befitting the devout search for inspiration upon it. Such hallowed ground is ruinously expensive to maintain. Pick up your feet when you walk to avoid tearing the fragile turf with your cleats. Even at the risk of keeping others waiting, never run across a green. If you must, run around it.

Leave bags and cart off the green, in the direction of the next tee.

HELLO, I MUST BE GOING

Approaching the green, whether by cart or on foot, before you do anything else, locate the next tee box. Anticipate your departure by placing clubs or carts off the green on the side nearest the next tee. This way, after everyone has holed out, you can exit the green en route to the next hole without having to retrace your steps.

PARKING IS PROHIBITED

Carts should be left on the cart path for a fast getaway, never abandoned in front of the green. Before you putt, pull the cart up as far as you can on the path, at least even with the green or, ideally, to the next tee. Should there be no ropes, yellow boundary stakes, or signs placed strategically around the green to prevent carts from approaching, you are still expected to obey common sense. Return the cart to the path. Never drive up to the green, onto the fringe, or, heaven forbid, onto the putting surface itself.

CHANGING PARTNERS

Situation: Your ball lies several yards short of the green on the opposite side from the next tee. Do you

1) Play your approach shot first, then, before you putt, carry and leave your clubs just off the green toward the next tee?

or

2) Deposit your clubs near the next tee and then walk back to play carrying your approach club and your putter?

Answer: Whichever's faster.

Clubs are often lost around the green when the approach club gives way to the putter. By setting the club down carefully on the "exit" side of the green or near the pulled flagstick, it will be harder to forget. Just make sure it's out of harm's way. Do not keep others waiting by making a separate trip over to the cart or bag to return the club or, worse, by flinging it in the bag's or cart's general direction.

Gloves also have a habit of disappearing around the green. Some players take them off to putt, others keep them on. If you do take them off, snap them around your approach club or make sure they are securely in your pocket.

"GREEN" CADDIES

The luxury of a caddy will allow you to concentrate on your putting. Times being what they are, however, it is not unusual to find a playing partner's son, daughter, nephew, etc., reluctantly pressed into caddy duty—a mixed blessing, to put it mildly.

A "green" caddy can be a veritable bull in a china shop on the putting green. Caddying is a noble institution that instills noble virtues, not the least of which is an insight into human nature. You are to be commended for seeking to pass the game and its wisdom on to future generations. We ask only that you consider the inconvenience to others.

The proper time to educate a caddy is not on Saturday morning or at any time when the course is at peak capacity. Unschooled caddies should observe and learn from the sidelines. Let everyone putt in peace. If the kids are not caddying but happen to be along for the ride, then there is no reason they should ever be on the green, where they will just be in the way.

THE SHORTEST DISTANCE BETWEEN TWO POINTS (AGAIN)

Putting lines, touched on in our discussion of the practice green, take on special significance on the course. We can't emphasize their importance enough. If you can do one thing on the putting green (in addition to sinking your putt) with respect to etiquette, be conscious of stepping on someone else's line.

Again, the putting line is an imaginary line that connects each ball with the hole. Walk around or step over them lightly, as if they were puddles threatening a white pair of shoes. Believe it or not, a footprint can alter the roll of the ball. Even if you are certain your step couldn't possibly affect the course of golfing history, observe the courtesy as a formality. Watch a tournament and you will see this unwritten rule followed to the letter of the law akin to the solemnity of the changing of the guard.

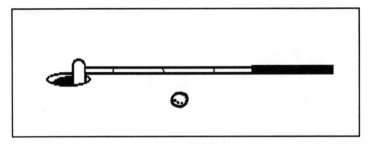

"Inside the leather."

Of course, accidents will happen. When they do, a brief, sincere, and instant apology should suffice. Your consideration may also enlighten others unaware that an apology was necessary or that putting lines even exist.

On short putts, you may have to straddle a line. If someone appears to be risking serious back injury contorting themselves to avoid stepping on your line, you can acknowledge their consideration and invite them to putt out. Courtesy has been served.

GIMME!

In casual play, gimmes are often allowed for putts close enough to assume their sinking is automatic. You'll often hear the remark *inside the leather* on putts left near the hole. A ball is inside the leather when it lies inside the grip when the putter is placed in the hole. It is a common benchmark for gimmes. Accepted only after it has been offered, a gimme still counts as one stroke.

THE DAMAGE YOU'VE DONE

A ball that hits the putting green on the fly will leave a mark that you are obligated to repair as best you can. With a tee or,

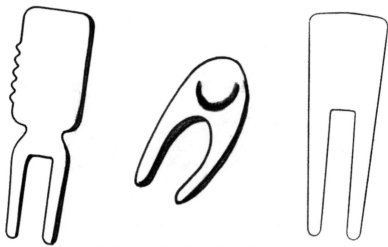

Tools for repairing the surface of the green.

better yet, a ball mark repairer, gently work around and under the depression, lifting it and turning inward in a circle until it is pushed up level with the grass around it. Then tap it down lightly with your putter.

It's easy to overlook repairing a ball mark when your ball hits the green on the fly and then starts rolling. Once it stops on the back of the green, no mark will be evident near the ball. But a mark may remain on the front of the green where the ball landed. It should not be overlooked.

This is the only way the putting green can be improved. Loose impediments such as twigs or leaves can be removed. You are not allowed, however, to smooth anything over or pat anything down.

CLOSEST IN TENDS THE PIN

In the absence of caddies, the player whose ball lies closest to the hole should tend the flagstick. Other players should find their balls, repair their own ball marks, and prepare to putt.

Tending the flagstick, or pin, is simply holding the shaft at arm's length from the hole. When the wind is blowing, hold the flag to keep it from flapping.

Beware of shadows. Your shadow and the pin's shadow should ideally be cast on the same side of the hole. Stand on the side of the flagstick that will allow this. Before a putt is actually struck, pull up on the pin gently; sometimes they're stuck in there pretty good. When the ball is struck, remove the pin. Don't wait for the ball to roll close.

The flagstick makes it easier to visually locate the cup. If no one wants it attended or all players are on the green, pull it, setting it down lightly out of the way (be sure to ask first rather than automatically pulling it). It needs to be placed far enough away from the hole so that a ball rolling well past the cup won't hit it.

How to repair a ball mark.

RULES TO PUTT BY

The rules change on the green. A ball is defined as on the green when any part of it touches the putting surface.

One reason the flagstick is placed well out of the way and removed quickly when attended is because if a putted ball from on the green hits it, it's a two-stroke penalty. (It's OK if you hit the pin from off the green.) When you are playing from just off the green, you have the option of leaving the flag in the cup. Sometimes it's advisable to do so, using the flag as a target to prevent the ball from rolling past. The decision to leave it in or pull it out is up to you.

A two-stroke penalty is also assessed if you putt your ball on the green into another ball on the green. Don't worry about any of this when your ball lies in the fairway or the bunker. From either location, there is no penalty if your ball strikes a ball on the green. If this does happen, the first ball (the one that was hit) should be replaced as close to its original position as possible. (Note: Other rules apply in tournament formats.)

MORE ADVICE AND DISSENT

On televised tournaments, you will hear professionals consulting with their caddies before a putt, talking about *left edge* or *right edge*. They are trying to figure out where to hit the ball, allowing for the contours of the green, or the *break*. As far as the rules are concerned, in team formats (see Chapter 8) you can ask the advice of your partners or caddy. In friendly games, you may seek help reading a putt providing no one physically points the way for you by touching the green.

Unsolicited advice about putts is better left unsaid. Keep your thoughts to yourself, unless you're asked for an opinion. Worst of all is the well-intentioned reminder. "Hey, Bill, sink this three footer and you'll break 90"—that sort of thing is taboo. If Bill has never broken 90 before, this is a certain jinx. For this reason, during a no-hitter in baseball everyone on the bench is forbidden from mentioning it out loud. Of course, they all know what is happening. In this instance, Bill certainly does not require any reminding. He knows darn well he needs the putt. Calling attention to it is terribly rude. Better to say nothing at all until after the fateful stroke, especially if you aren't certain of its significance.

It's not easy to follow your partners' every shot from tee to green, but try to keep an eye out for what happens. When someone is playing a hole well, asking "Is that for birdie?" may sound innocent enough, but it's a needless distraction. Better to hold off asking questions, especially if the player is over their ball and about to putt. The golfer oblivious to everything but his or her own ball and score is not much fun to play with. You don't have to be a fan, but a "nice putt" or a "tough break" will make the nice shots more enjoyable and the tough breaks easier to take.

MAKING YOUR MARK

A ball in your way on the green may be marked. Any player may ask another to mark his or her ball. Marking should never be treated as an imposition, simply as an act of courtesy. Don't be shy about asking. After all, you're risking the possibility of a two-stroke penalty should you hit another ball on the green.

You may mark your ball anytime it is on the green. Remember, you cannot pick your ball up without first marking it. If your ball obviously lies in someone's way, don't wait to be asked. Mark it. If you are not sure whether your ball is in the way, either mark it or leave it alone and wait to be asked. But don't ask. No matter how polite it sounds, "Do you want me to mark my ball?" is a needless interruption when someone is preparing to putt.

Any number of things can be used to adequately mark a ball: a coin, a button snapped from a golf glove, or a plastic disc designed for the purpose. (Please, no stray candy wrappers,

Attending the pin.

leaves, or a tee stuck in the ground.) There is a preferred way to mark a golf ball. The marker must be placed directly behind the ball in relation to the hole. Then the ball may be lifted. The most common mistake is to pick up the ball first and then put down a marker. Put down the mark first, then remove the ball.

To replace the ball, the sequence is reversed. Put the ball down first in front of the mark, then pick up the mark.

MOVING YOUR MARK

No one has to putt over a ball mark that might deflect a putt. The player putting directs to which side of the putting line the mark should be moved. To move a mark, first mark the ball. Then, place the putter head alongside the mark. Move the mark one putter-head length away from the original position. If the green has a big break in it, this may have to be done several times over. The one stipulation is that the mark must be replaced before the ball can be returned to its original position. It isn't as complicated as it sounds. Occasionally, instead of marking, the player farthest from the hole may offer those in front of him or her the opportunity to *putt out,* or go before, to save time.

FARTHEST AWAY, FIRST TO PLAY

As on the fairway, the same order generally applies to the putting green: the player farthest from the hole plays first. If two balls seem equidistant from the hole, the person tending the flag determines who is away or out. The person who is out putts first.

Situation: Which ball is away?

a) A ball on the green 30 feet from the cup?
or
b) A ball off the green 10 feet from the cup?

Answer: (a). The ball farthest from the hole wherever that is—on the fairway, in a bunker, or on the other side of the putting green—is said to be away. *A* plays first.

There is one preferred way to mark a golf ball.

CONTINUOUS PUTTING

Marking and replacing balls admittedly takes time. One way to speed up play on the green without sacrificing anything but time is the green equivalent to ready golf, continuous putting.

Continuous putting simply means that instead of taking turns, once a player starts putting, he or she continues until their ball is in the cup. We encourage it in recreational play. Turn taking is actually enforced by the rules only in certain competitive formats.

OUT OF SIGHT, OUT OF MIND

Francis Ouimet would go on to win the 1913 U.S. Open in a titanic upset, but when he came to the 17th green, he desperately needed to sink a snaking fifteen-foot downhill putt for a birdie. So intense was his concentration, Ouimet recalled, that he never heard the car horns blaring from a traffic jam directly behind the green.

Some golfers are like that. They can putt placidly through trains, planes, automobile accidents, or building demolitions. Then there are others, like the P. G. Wodehouse character who blamed his missed putts on the "uproar of the butterflies in the adjoining meadows."

Most golfers fall somewhere in between. Richard Francis could have been speaking for many when he wrote, "Among my many idiosyncracies is the havoc whispers cause me when I have taken my stance, especially to putt. A passing train, the chimes of a nearby church are nothing; but the low murmur of a voice upsets my nerves and disposition, which is bad enough at best, and more often than not ruins the shot." The big sounds no one can do anything about, but the whispering and coin jingling, that's something else.

When others are putting, courtesy requires you to stand as unobtrusively as possible. This means out of their direct line of sight, not directly in front of or behind them, even if you are standing off the green. Readjust your position a few steps one way or the other as required.

Talking is permissible until a player addresses his or her putt. Just as on the tee, when the player is over the ball, that is the signal to be quiet. If you are not in position behind your ball when someone begins the address, hold still until after the putt. Do not walk across the green while someone is putting.

SHOOT YOUR SHOT

Being in position and ready to play, as elsewhere on the course, is important on the green. The meter is running. Practice putts, impromptu lessons, and putting after play is completed all slow down the game.

When a ball stops rolling, the light has changed. It is someone else's turn to go. Allow the absolute minimum for color commentary, four-part analysis, and instant replays. Step up and play. Again, this will send a message to others to keep play moving. Naturally, if you've just blown a three footer for par, you'll want to hole it a few times to regain your self-respect. If—and this is a big if—no one is pressing from behind, you may do so after everyone has putted out for their real score.

It may seem obvious, but when you sink your putt, retrieve it from the hole before anyone else plays. The sound of a ball striking the cup is one to be savored unimpeded by another ball.

EXIT STAGE LEFT

The first person to sink his or her putt should retrieve and replace the flagstick after the last person holes out. This avoids the unfortunate scenario of leaving one poor soul to sink a three footer, replace the pin, collect his or her clubs, and then scamper off to the tee like the Mad Hatter.

Be careful replacing the flagstick. The most fragile area of the green, and thus the most easily damaged, is the area surrounding the cup. Carelessness can be especially destructive. Leave it secure in its mooring, pointing straight up.

Leaving the green together helps the flow of traffic. It gives a clear signal to players waiting in the fairway that it is safe to play. Because carts and clubs have been left to the side rather than the front of the green, players behind you have an unobstructed view to decide what club to use and can be ready to play as soon as you are out of the picture.

ANY BIRDIES?

Once you are off the green, you'll have ample opportunity to record your score. Another cardinal sin is to pull out your card and begin tallying up while others are still putting or players are waiting to play behind you. It's like starting dessert while your companion is still working on the entree. Don't pull out the pencil or obviously begin counting your strokes until play is completed.

CHAPTER SEVEN CHECKLIST

___ "Park" clubs, carts on exit side of green.
___ Discard clubs on the green where you can see them.
___ Only players and (trained) caddies belong on the green.
___ Walk over and around putting lines.
___ Repair ball marks.
___ Closest to the hole tends the pin.
___ Attend pin on the side where the shadow is cast.
___ Pull the flagstick when the putt is struck.

___ Mark your ball from behind only.
___ Be ready to play when it's your turn.
___ Take your ball out of the hole after you sink it.
___ First to hole out retrieves and replaces the flagstick.
___ Leave the green together.

CHAPTER SEVEN GLOSSARY

Birdie—One shot less than par.
Bogey—One shot over par.
Break—The contours of the green, which affect the roll of a ball.
Double Bogey—Two shots over (or above) par.
Eagle—Two shots under (or less than) par.
Fringe—The close-cut grass that surrounds the green. Also known as the apron, frog hair, or collar.
Inside the Leather—Slang expression for a gimme.
Lag—A long putt played close to, but short of, the hole.
Left Edge, Right Edge—The sides of the cup used as targets.
Makable—A putt with a good chance of being made.
Missable—A putt that's easy to miss.
Par—Determined by yardage, the regulation number of strokes set for a hole played perfectly.
Pitch or Chip In—A shot that goes directly into the hole from off the green.
Out—Slang for "away." The ball farthest from the hole.
Putt Out—To hole out or putt the ball in the hole.
Triple Bogey—Three shots over par.

8

IN THE CLUBHOUSE

WHILE THE OBJECTIVE of golf is universal—"to hit a very small ball into an even smaller hole, with weapons singularly ill-designed for the purpose" (an opinion often attributed to Winston Churchill)—you'll find the game means different things to different people. Not everyone takes up or plays the game for the same reasons. Potentially awkward situations beyond the basics of play and conduct await the uninitiated. The sanctuary of the clubhouse provides a proper setting to cover these advanced aspects of golf that can be as mystifying as they are inevitable.

SHOP TALK

Industrialists Charles Schwab and Andrew Carnegie may have started golf's reputation as a major player in the art of the deal. Over a round nearly 100 years ago, the two moguls got to talking. By the 18th hole, Carnegie had agreed to sell out to J. P. Morgan, paving the way for the formation of a little outfit called U.S. Steel. Business and golf have been as cozy as Scotch and water ever since. Whether deals are made on the golf course as often as everyone thinks, the opportunity to mix business with golfing pleasure is increasingly familiar up and down the corporate ladder. But away from the office, "set down on nature's everlasting pages," to quote the Bard, some golfers clearly resent having their golf sullied with trivial (that is, non-golf-related) matters, especially subjects as unpleasant as work.

William Howard Taft, a president who diligently refused to let the rigors of office interfere with his game, believed, "The beauty of golf is that you cannot play if you permit yourself to think of anything else." For many officeholders and office dwellers alike, that sums up golf's allure to a tee.

On the course, golf should top the agenda. The only relevant pitch you should be concerned with making is the one that will leave you *dead* to the pin. Leave networking to drinks at the 19th hole or, if and when, your client broaches the subject first. At Augusta National in Georgia, the fabled home of the Masters Tournament, the captains of industry who make up the membership are actually forbidden—in writing—from shop talk of any kind on club grounds.

The possibility exists, of course, that a good shot can pay off on the bottom line as well as on the scorecard. It did for Willie Turnesa, an accomplished amateur champion who often played with corporate clients. A hot prospect once made him the following proposition: reach the green of a long par 3 with a 3-iron, and a $300,000 account is yours. The ball landed on the green, and the account landed in Willie's pocket.

"If you're going to have to buy from someone," Herbert Warren Wind wrote, "you might as well give your business to a guy who can treat you to a succession of first-class golf shots." Willie's blue-chip duffer would probably agree.

Even if no business results, at the very least the golf course remains an excellent place to observe human behavior. Looking back on a lifetime of golf, Willie Turnesa reflected that "through golf you get to know the insides of people." Or as sportswriter Thomas Boswell writes in his insightful book *Strokes of Genius*: "Golf may not teach character, but it reveals it."

HANDICAPS

Not having a handicap becomes a handicap itself the more golf you play. Word games aside, a handicap is important. It levels the playing field, allowing players of all abilities to compete together legitimately, the same as it does in league bowling. A handicap is golf's calling card, recognized wherever the game is played. You needn't feel you have to be a "good" golfer (whatever that is) to have one.

Handicaps are established using legitimate scores (counting all strokes played by the rules). Local associations or clubs do the paperwork for a nominal fee: tallying scores, posting revisions, arranging handicap tournaments. To be included, scorecards must be signed, or *attested,* by a member of your foursome and turned in at the clubhouse.

In layman's terms, a handicap is the average of the best ten out of twenty scores recorded. The equation gets complicated when indices such as *slope* and par are figured in, which naturally differ from one course to the next.

Your handicap might be lower on an easy course and higher on a difficult course. A USGA study once determined that the majority of golfers shoot one to three strokes above their handicap. If that's true, on a par-70 course, a 15-handicapper probably shoots between 87 and 90; a 20- between 92 and 95.

Over a lifetime, handicaps are subject to the vagaries of golf and life; as with stock markets, periodic adjustments are made for inflation and recession. Professionals hover around zero or lightly on the plus side (a plus 4, for instance, is four strokes better than scratch). The maximum handicap, given to absolute beginners, is 36. The lower the handicap, the better the golfer.

The only way to determine an honest handicap is to turn in honest scores, good and bad. We strongly advise it. Some players prefer to stand only by their better scores. Their reward is a dubious one: an inaccurate handicap.

There are also villians known as *sandbaggers,* who only turn in their high scores. This is done deliberately, to secure a dishonest edge in tournaments. With a higher and inflated handicap, they receive more strokes than they otherwise deserve, winning prizes unfairly. Oddly enough, these scoundrels acquire notoriety, but not much is ever done about them.

Two definitions: *gross* score is the actual score shot; *net* score is the total after adjustments for handicap. A gross score might be 101, but with a 15 handicap, the net score is 86.

Social and charity events often award prizes for best gross and net scores. There are also other awards, some for unfortunate distinctions such as shortest drive and most putts on a hole. It's all in good fun. USGA, PGA, and LPGA (Ladies Professional Golf Association) tournaments are always gross scoring events. To even try to qualify for the men's U.S. Open, for example, your handicap cannot be higher than 2.

IF YOU'RE SCORING AT HOME

On the scorecard under HOLE, YARDAGE, and PAR, an additional column, HANDICAP, appears, followed by a series of numbers. The numbers correspond to the difficulty rating of each hole compared with the rest of the course. The most difficult hole on the front nine is the number one handicap hole. The most difficult hole on the back nine is the number two. The system alternates from front to back until all eighteen holes are rated.

What does it all mean? Say you're playing a match with a friend and there is a handicap difference of five between you. (Your handicap is 15, hers is 20). Your friend will receive five strokes, but, much as she might like, she is not afforded the luxury of taking them whenever and wherever she chooses. Instead, every hole handicapped one through five indicates a *stroke hole*, where the awarded strokes apply, perhaps holes 3, 5, 8, 12, and 13.

For the purposes of the match, you will count your true score. But on those holes specified on the scorecard, your friend

Hole	COURSE RATING MEN	WOMEN	1	2	3	4	5	6	7	8	9	Out
Red	64.5	69.0	304	78	398	226	333	304	400	75	287	2,405
White	67.5	72.9	313	138	474	252	367	352	450	113	330	2,789
Blue	70.1		346	170	490	283	387	372	498	142	350	3,038
Gold	73.4		393	192	515	310	441	438	515	152	366	3,322
CLUB NUMBER OR GUEST	Men's Handicap		12	16	6	10	2	8	4	18	14	
	Par		4	3	5	4	4	4	5	3	4	36
	Ladies Handicap		7	15	5	13	3	9	1	17	11	

10	11	12	13	14	15	16	17	18	In	Total	Hdcp	Net
303	287	314	86	275	426	104	428	340	2,563	4,968		
351	354	346	109	284	489	123	451	361	2,868	5,657		
373	370	364	120	350	539	154	485	408	3,136	6,174		
396	446	432	160	358	552	205	510	441	3,500	6,822		
9	7	1	17	11	5	15	13	3				
4	4	4	3	4	5	3	5	4	36	72		
12	10	2	18	14	4	16	6	8				

Player
Course Played
Attest
Date

Sample scorecard.

gets to deduct one stroke from her actual score. Say you shoot a 5 and your friend *cards* a 6. The hole is then said to be *halved*, or tied. If you both score 5s, then your friend, by virtue of the free stroke, wins the hole. All the other holes are played straight. Another way an excellent player can play evenly with a high-handicapper is simply by deducting the difference in strokes at the end of the round.

TOURNAMENT TIME

Tournaments are the next floor up on golf's mental and competitive escalator. You too can suffer the pangs of "needing" a three footer, even if it is only a vicarious thrill compared with what the pros experience.

There are myriad formats, aside from *stroke,* or *match play*. *Best balls* and *scrambles* record a foursome's lowest score in different ways. In scrambles, all players tee off. The best shot of the four is selected. The other players move their balls, and everyone plays on from the best drive position. Play continues with the best shot out of the four as the ball in play until the hole is completed. Birdie opportunities abound with four tries on every shot. Someone will probably hit it close, which explains why winning scores are usually quite low, into the high 50s or low 60s. A beginner with a hot putter can really contribute in a scramble.

Best balls, with handicaps included, count the lowest score recorded by an individual team member on every hole. A high handicapper who birdies a par 3 gives his or her team the equivalent of a hole-in-one: for him or her, a par counts as a birdie. Best balls or scrambles can be either two-person or four-person affairs. Teams can also be picked by pairing A, B, C, & D players together, again using handicaps as a bench mark.

Many social or charity tournaments are *shotgun* starts. Play begins with teams starting on every hole, rather than solely on number one, as in more formal events. The advantage is that everyone starts and finishes at approximately the same time, if not at the same place.

HOWDY, STRANGER

Chances are good that sooner or later, if you play the social or charity events, you'll be paired with a stranger. Playing for yourself is hard enough. No one used to care about your four-putts, but now you've got a partner or three. It adds a new dimension to the game and to that old bugaboo—advice. Those too quick with it—even with the best interests of the team at heart—would do well to remember that the road to hell is paved with good intentions.

In a typical charity event, expectations will vary within the foursome. Two players are probably just out to have a good time; one player will be hell-bent on victory, and the other player may not be entirely sure why he or she is there.

It can present some problems. How to head them off? You might try the approach of Horton Smith, a pro in the 1930s who was said to begin his round by shaking hands with his partner (always a good start). He'd say how glad he was with the *pairing*, then add, "I'm apologizing right now for any mistakes that I make today, but this is my last apology. Now let's go out there and do our best."

Another tack, culled from a country club bulletin board, reads in part:

> You are my partner for today, not by choice. I probably got you in a blind draw or perhaps nothing better was available. I think I know what the objective of the game is. So Please . . .

> Don't tell me to take my time on any putts.
> Don't tell me to knock it in.
> Don't tell me to get it up there.
> Don't tell me we need this.

> IF I WANT ANY ADVICE I WILL ASK FOR IT. SO UP UNTIL THAT TIME, KEEP YOUR DAMNED MOUTH SHUT.

PLAYING "FOR A LITTLE SOMETHING"

Handicaps also come in handy picking up sides in less formal settings. Figuring out how many strokes should be given would seem fairly easy, but thoughtful and spirited bargaining often results. Offers may be received with the distaste of a labor negotiator reviewing management's latest concessions. Depending upon what transpires on the course, jokes, taunts, and occasionally bad feelings can result. These can last a few holes, the rest of the round, until the next round, or, quite possibly, for the rest of your life.

The low handicapper always complains about having to give away too many strokes; the high handicapper never thinks he or she gets enough. One thing's for certain: whether it is better to give than to receive is a question most golfers have no trouble coming to grips with. Give them a couple of bogeys and old friends can start on each other like combatants in joint counseling. "You're getting heavy, Bill. You hear me? I'm not a friggin' camel. Come on, babe. I can't carry you forever." And so it goes.

The cause of all the commotion, to no one's surprise, is the root of all evil. The bottom line may be as little as fifty cents, but a bet is still a bet.

Golf and betting go way back, as early Scottish club records confirm. For some, golf is just not worth the effort if it's not played "for a little something." Those little somethings can add up. Sam Snead tells a story about Bobby Riggs in the early 1950s. Playing $1,000 *nassaus* with an oilman, Riggs walked away at the end of the week with almost $200,000 in his pockets. Nice work, if you can get it.

There are an infinite number of ways to gamble at golf. It can be all consuming. The story is often told of the player who canters down the fairway swelled with visions and quick calculations of bets past, present and future. But, wait. There's a problem. Out in the fairway, he can't find his ball. The foursome scours the rough to no avail until . . . someone realizes: The reason the ball isn't in the fairway is because it's still on the tee. He forgot to tee off! President Warren Harding, an inveterate golfer who tried to teach his dog to retrieve practice balls on the south lawn of the White House, routinely had so many bets going he had a Secret Service man keep the books.

There are many potential pitfalls in betting on anything, especially golf, not the least of which is severing a friendship. Doug Sanders, a man who knows something of the subject, suggests the following advice:

> Never gamble to hurt a friend.
> Never gamble outside your comfort zone.
> Never needle, harass, or poke fun at a playing partner on the edge of despair.
> Never fail to settle your debts immediately after a round. If you win, be gracious.

A FEW POINTS OF REFERENCE

Bets can be made between individuals, partners, or teams. Rather than rely on the score for the entire round, *matches* provide a means to bet on every hole. Betting games may differ by region, club, or foursome, but there are some universal basics.

A nassau is actually three bets. The first is for the best score on the front nine holes, the second for the best score on the back nine holes, the third for the winning eighteen-hole score. In a straight two-dollar nassau, the most you could lose would be six dollars. But a nassau can be just the overture.

Pressing commonly makes things more interesting. After one team loses (usually) two holes, pressing means an additional bet begins on the next hole. It can be called or become automatic depending on the conditions set in the clubhouse or on the first tee.

Drop three holes and your balance sheet reads: three holes down on the first bet and, because of the press, one hole down on the second bet. Lose another hole and you will be four holes down on the first bet, two on the second (with a press on for the next hole). Win the next hole and you are now three holes down on the first bet, one down on the second, and now one up on the third bet. Now you know why Warren Harding kept a Secret Service agent with a sharp pencil handy.

If you are going to allow automatic presses, make sure you have enough money to cover a disaster; the bets can multiply like bunnies. A two-dollar nassau with presses, individual, team, and other side bets can balloon to sixty dollars or more.

The popular skins format goes like this: a *skin* is won when a player wins a hole; if two or more players tie, then all tie, and the pot (it can be as little as a dime a hole) rolls over to the next hole and keeps getting larger until someone records a skin.

Another popular game is Bingle, Bangle, Bongle. Points are awarded: one for the first player to reach the green (bingle); one for the closest shot to the hole (bangle); one for the first in the hole once everyone is on the green (bongle).

Matches inside matches honor brilliant strokes: birdies, eagles, chip-ins from off the green, getting down in two (strokes) from a bunker, you name it. If someone says on the first tee that they want to play all the goodies or trash, such as greenies (closest to the pin on par 3s), sandies (up and down from a bunker), barkies (hit a tree and still make par), *Arnies* (a par without ever being on the fairway), etc., etc., before agreeing, you better find out what the heck they're talking about. With so many different games going, if you intend to become one of the gang, it behooves you to become familiar with the ones played most often.

PAYING OFF

For most golfers, but not all, it is not the money. It's the principle of the thing. Even if the payoff is in nickels, paying up is considered a point of honor. It is excruciatingly bad form to walk away from a bet, calling to question your basic integrity and character. If you don't intend to take it seriously, better to not get involved in the first place.

Undoubtedly, we'd all be better off taking the advice of James

Bond's nemesis Auric Goldfinger, who noted the safest way to double your money is to fold it up and put it back in your pocket.

CHEATING

Speaking of that notorious golf hustler, it was in his famous match with Special Agent 007 that cheating has never been more fiendishly practiced or ingeniously parried. Cheating is very easy in golf. Deliberately recording a 5 instead of a 6 on the scorecard, improving a ball's lie in the rough, replacing a marked ball closer to the hole—there are a million and one other effortless infractions that no one is likely to catch.

For those who apply themselves to it, like Goldfinger, cheating at golf is child's play. His ball buried in a cavernous sand bunker, the fictitious villian jumped into the sand, landing on either side of his ball. The effect was to pinch the sand in such a way as to tee up his ball for an easy escape.

Several distinctions need to be made about cheating. First, it must be defined. Cheating is the deliberate intent to deceive. It is not an oversight, an accident, or a simple misunderstanding of the rules. It is done on purpose.

Another distinction must be made between recreational play and tournament play. In a friendly game, the participants decide how closely they will adhere to the rules. If wagers are involved, no matter how small, everyone should at least play by the same rules, even if they aren't strictly USGA. Some social events, to raise more funds for charity, sell Mulligans at five or ten dollars a pop, limit two per customer. There is nothing wrong with playing them—as long as everyone can.

What should you do when someone cheats to win a bet? Confrontation won't resolve it. Your only effective recourse is to avoid playing, or wagering, with that person again.

In formal tournaments, with respect to the rules, there are no degrees of honesty. An infraction either occurred or it didn't. Like pregnancy, there are no in-betweens, no gray areas.

In casual rounds, the only person really being cheated is the person who cheats. If other players want to improve their lie, play winter rules, or turn a blind eye toward a *chili dip* or two, that's their business. If they choose to write down par when you know double figures are more like it, what difference does it make to you or anyone else?

In competitions, however, cheating victimizes the whole field. Everyone else in the tournament, diligently following the rules to the letter, is impacted. Remember again that in golf, each player shares officiating responsibilities. If you notice a violation and do nothing about it, you are also at fault. In social or charity events in which teams are allowed to choose their own partners, cheating can take on a partylike atmosphere. Playing for a good cause, however, doesn't justify bending the rules. The complicity of the group is no excuse. It is each player's obligation, as unpleasant as it may be, to ensure that the tournament is played fairly. Anything else is dishonest, whether it's the Eastside Lions Club Halloween Best Ball or the PGA Championship. If you feel uncomfortable about confronting others, report it to the pro at either the turn or the end of the round.

There are, however, several advantages to bringing it up right then and there: 1) the player may not be aware that he or she cheated, and 2) nipping it in the bud prevents the transgression from being repeated. It also gives the player an opportunity to rectify the error in context: they might play another ball, for instance, rather than risk disqualification later, when it's too late to do anything about it.

Rules disputes can be settled immediately with a ruling or by playing out two balls to the satisfaction of the disputing parties, as Arnold Palmer did at the Masters. The pro will sort it out later.

Golf isn't a matter of life or death, but, by the same token, honesty is not just something that we practice in life for the sake of convenience. A golfer is only as good as his or her word.

New players need not fear accusations of cheating. Teeing up the ball in the fairway or other training-wheel-type advantages are permissible—as long as every attempt to play in a timely manner is made.

As your proficiency at golf moves beyond the beginning stages, we recommend the goal of strict adherence to the rules. There is an undeniable inner sense of satisfaction that comes from knowing you've done something the right way. Every golfer savors the accomplishment of having successfully pulled off a tough shot, as the ball lies, as the game was intended. It's a great feeling. That's what golf is all about.

PLAYING WITH MORE EXPERIENCED PLAYERS

Unlike tennis, in which each player's ability is essential to the game—if you can't keep the ball in the court, it's not going to be much fun, is it?—golf is different. In golf, what one player does is, for all intents and purposes, immaterial to another.

Your game may alternately show flashes of brilliance and exasperating displays of futility, but your knowledge and application of the Rules of Etiquette should never vary. As we hope you'll discover, they will serve you well no matter whom you play with, or where.

When you are playing with "better" players—whether that means someone who can break 100 or someone who can shoot par—everyone will have a better time if you observe the following guidelines:

On the first tee, stifle your understandable feeling of intimidation. Resist the temptation to explain or apologize before you've begun. There is no need to discuss how long it's been since you played, your lingering war wounds, or the accumulating stress of your roofing problems. Everyone's got problems; that's why they're out on the golf course in the first place. Yours are best kept to yourself. Your golf ailments will no doubt be apparent soon enough anyway.

Patronizing conversation is also unwelcome. "You won't enjoy playing with me. I'll slow you down. I'm not nearly as good as you are. I'll ruin your game, etc., etc." No one should have to be saddled with the additional burden of someone else's psychological needs. It's distracting, not to mention embarrassing and exhausting, to have to buoy a stranger's ego and self-esteem.

Complimenting your playing partners for their good shots is welcome, but explaining your misses isn't. Subjected to a steady diet of listening to you degrade your swing, shots, fate, and the undesirability of having you along in the first place, the more experienced player may feel obligated to offer reassurances. This distracts him or her from the game. Avoid beating a dead horse. Know when it's your turn, keep an eye out for other people's shots and putting lines, and play in a timely fashion, and you should be all right.

When you compliment someone for a good shot, make certain it is in fact a good shot. A hook or a slice may look good at first, before it takes a turn for the worst. As with bad shots, when someone gives you a compliment, no excuses or detailed explanations are required. Thank them.

If it becomes obvious that you are slowing the group down, step on the accelerator. Hustle to your ball, take only one practice swing, or none at all, and occasionally pick up in moments of frustration and start fresh on the next hole. You will garner respect, despite your woes, if you can play without being told what to do and when to do it.

When you get to the green, if you're putting for 6s, 7s, or 8s, get it over with quickly. Don't waste time lining up your putts. The pros do many things differently from the rest of us. One of them is putt. Their painstaking deliberations on the greens give novices a mistaken impression. As we'll see in the next chapter, the pros have their reasons for doing what they do, some of them quite compelling. But especially in situations where you are not as accomplished as the other players, don't dawdle. Keep up, keep up, keep up.

You may have observed that experienced players are not always perfect when it comes to etiquette. Good manners don't necessarily go with successfully hitting a golf ball. Golf demands high ethical standards of its players, as well as athletic prowess. Those players accomplished at all facets of the game, including sportsmanship, are the ones held in highest esteem.

Playing with better players is an opportunity to glimpse the possibility of playing well. With a little experience under your belt and the knowledge of what is expected of you, you'll find it can be pleasant for all concerned.

PLAYING IN A PRO–AM

It may be hard for the rest of us to believe, but to the touring professional golf is just a job. It's a great job, none better, but it's still a job. Top-level golf requires the same commitment and determination as achieving success in any field. If most of us have an idyllic view of what the pros go through, at least in part, it's understandable. Turn on the TV some snowy Sunday. Where are the golfers? Hawaii, Florida, or somewhere else where the weather is perfect and the surroundings undeniably beautiful. And what are they doing? They're playing golf, for goodness sake. What could be easier? Everything's taken care of. All they have to do is make their tee time. The only heavy lifting is done by the caddies.

What the public doesn't see is all the hours the pros put in, the years of struggle, the anxiety. We see only the good times, the highlights. For us, golf is diversion, recreation, a few laughs. For the pros, it's all consuming, their livelihoods, serious business.

At every pro event, a Pro–Am (which is rarely televised) precedes the actual tournament. It gives the sponsors, their clients, and prospects a public relations return on their investment for helping defray the tournament expenses. The payoff for them is in PR and corporate goodwill. To a select chosen few, it takes the form of a round of golf with an honest-to-goodness professional golfer.

For the amateur, the opportunity may be the golfing highlight of the year, a chance to rub shoulders with the game's elite. For the pro, however, it is a down day, an obligation. With the amateur's expectations sky-high and the pro on automatic pilot, confusion and cross-purposes are inevitable.

The typical format has the pro playing for a money prize. He will adhere strictly to the rules. The other players will be teamed according to handicap and the best ball of the foursome will compete against the rest of the field. The pro will hit from the back tees, the ones he or she will play in the tournament. The amateurs don't.

The presence of a pro, the charged air of a tournament, the smattering of a gallery can all induce an acute outbreak of nerves. Of course, the contrast with the pros is profound. For them, it's a social obligation, a warm-up. They've got nothing to be nervous about. After all, this is their office. The pressure won't start until the tournament does. They've also been playing golf in front of large crowds for some time.

Al Geiberger has played in Pro–Ams for three decades, on the PGA Tour and Senior Tour. He suggests that Pro–Am participants realize that the pro doesn't expect them to play as well as he does. Don't fret over missed shots. Probably what annoys pros the most is the same thing that bugs you and me out on the local muni: slow play. Extend the courtesies you've worked hard to hone. If your score is approaching double digits, pick up your ball.

To help neutralize terror on the first tee, Geiberger suggests keeping one *swing thought* in mind. Keep it simple. Keep your eye on the ball or relax. It also wouldn't hurt to learn a little about the pro with whom you'll be playing; where he or she is from, his or her family, favorite courses—the better to have something to talk about as you walk the course. You don't have to memorize the pro's tournament record, just be able to make conversation. And please don't try to wow the pro with a thorough account of your stunning victory in the Labor Day Best Ball at the club.

The professionals will be tactful about rule violations. They don't want to be in the position of admonishing someone who has contributed a lot of money to support the tournament. But don't hesitate or be embarrassed to ask about a rules interpretation. The pro will undoubtedly know the answer.

Finally, there are those who are dissatisfied unless they get a choice pairing with a headline pro. They spoil a potentially pleasant experience and the chance to compare notes with someone who is or once was near the pinnacle of their profession. Just because someone isn't a leading money winner doesn't mean he or she doesn't know their stuff or can't be an interesting and insightful companion for a round of golf.

CHAPTER EIGHT CHECKLIST

___ Leave networking to the 19th hole. On the course, golf should top the agenda.

___ "Golf may not teach character, but it reveals it."

___ Establish a handicap, golf's calling card.

___ Turn in all your scores, good *and* bad.

___ Familiarize yourself with basic betting terms.

___ Fast pay makes fast friends.

___ Cheating is the deliberate intent to deceive.

___ Rules disputes should be settled by the pro.

___ With better players, resist the temptation to explain or apologize.

CHAPTER EIGHT GLOSSARY

Attested—Signed.

Best Ball—Competition format in which teams record the best score on each hole.

Blind Hole Tournament—Format in which scores are culled from any nine of the eighteen holes.

Cards—Slang for scores, or records, as in "He carded a 5."

Chili Dip—Slang for a flubbed shot that takes too much turf and barely moves the ball.

Dead—Slang for a shot that lands near the hole. Also, stiff.

Flag Tournament—With handicaps in force, players continue until they use up the number of strokes in their handicaps. The player who plays the most golf wins.

Gross—Actual score shot during a round.

Halved—Tied.

Low Ball/Low Total—Tournament format in which one point is awarded on each hole for the low individual score and one point for the low team score.

Matches—Bets.

Match Play—Competition format determined by holes rather than strokes.

Nassau—A three-part bet: one for the winning total on the front nine, one for the winning total on the back nine, and one for the total score.

Net—Score after a handicap has been deducted from the gross score.

Pairing—When two players are scheduled to play together, though not necessarily as partners.

Press—Doubling the bet.

Pro–Am—Tournament format pairing professionals with amateurs.

Sandbagger—Golfer who fraudulently maintains a high handicap to gain unfair advantage during competition.

Scotch Foursome—Tournament format in which team members play one ball, alternating shots.

Scramble—Competition format in which teams choose the best shot as the ball in play.

Shotgun Start—Teams start on each hole rather than all tee off from the first hole.

Skin—Betting game in which the lowest score on a hole wins. If two tie, all tie, and the pot rolls over until someone records a skin, winning a hole outright.

Slope—Refinement to the handicap system, it adjusts handicaps to the difficulty of individual courses.

Stroke Hole—Hole where stroke is awarded according to handicap.

Stroke Play—Competition format in which total strokes determine the winner.

Swing Thought—An easy-to-remember aid to hitting the ball.

9

FEELING COMFORTABLE IN GOLF

SMELLING THE FLOWERS

ONE OF GOLF'S most enduring gifts is the pleasure it can bring away from the course. Pleasant diversions and discoveries that (thankfully) transcend ability await the curious and intrepid.

Many golfers unfortunately never look beyond the scorecard. Everyone wants to play well, but for those of us unwilling or unable to dedicate our life to the pursuit of golf perfection, Walter Hagen's famous advice still rings true: "Don't hurry. Don't worry. You're only here on a short visit, so don't forget to stop and smell the flowers."

Stopping to smell golf's flowers can take many forms. Savoring a single malt Scotch after a naturally rainy round on one of Scotland's famous (or not so famous) courses; the thrill of the hunt for collectibles; watching one of the most famous names in golf practice six-foot putts; it can even be as simple as turning on the television or opening a book.

Despite the game's permanence, golf has a history of invention and ingenuity that continues today. Take tees, for example. New Jersey dentist Dr. William Lowell is usually credited with first whittling little wooden pegs into tees. But what did golfers do before the humble tee? They (or more likely, their caddies) grabbed a handful of sand from a bucket on the teeing ground and formed little molehills. In 1895, a sand mold was patented. Instead of soiling their hands, golfers could now stamp and press the sand into a perfectly formed mound. Steel and even folded paper tees were tried. Driving-range mats still use a variation of a rubber tee patented more than a hundred years ago. And we're still not finished with the tee, as the search for a more ecologically benign alternative continues.

If the derivation of the tee doesn't interest you, other nooks and crannies abound. At the very least, your finds will impress your friends. Golf writer Charles Price wrote:

> Now people begin to look at you in a different light. You may have just played the course in a score resembling an area code, but suddenly the others in your foursome know your real game must be much better, or should be, and they blame today's miserable performance on an attack of Sciatica or something else you just didn't bother complaining about. You have become a truer golfer, somebody who has felt obligated to become knowledgeable about things the rest of us take for granted.

Golf lends itself to a good story, which helps explain why the game has attracted so many outstanding storytellers. Even Shakespeare, with a little imagination, may have taken a turn or two on the links as such lines as "Good words are better than bad strokes" and "O, cursed be the hand that made these holes!" suggest (*Julius Caesar,* 5.1, and *Richard III,* 1.2, respectively).

HITTING THE BOOKS

Nothing has ruined more golf swings than the myth of keeping the head down and the left arm straight (yes, we did say "myth"). If golf had reached the American West earlier, buckboard barkers might have been selling books with titles such as *Quick Draw;*

Slow Backswing and *The Wagon Wheel Approach to Curing a Slice* along with magic elixirs.

Of course, not all golf books are devoted to instruction. And many of the ones that are, are very good; that's why they're still in circulation decades after they were first published. Instruction titles share bookstore shelves with lavish coffee-table collections of course architecture, travel guides, record books, biographies, humor, and history.

While any arbitrary list is just that, we thought you might like to know some of the books that many golfers consider to be good reads or especially instructive. Public libraries are an excellent source not only for newer books but also for books long out of print. If you know what to ask for, interlibrary loan can also be an excellent resource for discovering wonderful books, often first editions, as the authors of this book discovered, to their delight.

Many great golf stories appear in collections such as *Press Box* by Red Smith (1976) and *The Omnibus of Sport* (1932) or in annual *Best Sports Stories* collections. Every year, the USGA offers a special limited printing of a forgotten gem. There is even a Book-of-the-Month-type club for golf.

Easier Said Than Done (instruction):
Harvey Penick's Little Red Book, Harvey Penick with Bud Schrake, 1992
A Round of Golf with Tommy Armour, Tommy Armour, 1959
Bobby Jones on Golf, Robert Tyre Jones, 1966
Five Lessons: The Modern Fundamentals of Golf, Ben Hogan & Herbert Warren Wind, 1957
How to Play Consistent Golf, Tom Kite, 1990
On Learning Golf, Percy Boomer, 1946

History, Humor, et al:
A History of Golf, Robert Browning, 1955
Back Then: A Pictorial History of American Golf, 1990
The Complete Golfer, ed. by Herbert Warren Wind, 1954
The Dogged Victims of Inexorable Fate, Dan Jenkins, 1970

Gettin' to the Dance Floor, Al Barkow, 1986
Golf in the Making, Ian T. Henderson & David I. Stirk, 1979
The Golf Omnibus, P. G. Wodehouse, 1973
Golfer-at-Large, Charles Price, 1982
Strokes of Genius, Thomas Boswell, 1989

MAKING IT LOOK EASY

Videos leave little to the imagination. Just take the club back like this—and presto. Nothing to it, right? Many golf videos are well produced, entertaining, sometimes humorous, even instructive. The more you watch, the more nuances of the game you'll pick up, as well as some terminology. But don't be discouraged if the shot doesn't come as easily to you as it appears to come to the pro in the video. Pros work on these shots diligently every day, as if their (professional) life depended on it. Remember, too: the mis-hits ended up on the cutting-room floor.

Many videos feature touring professionals long on marquee value but short on teaching skills. It's all well and good for pros to assume their audience understands what they mean by *pronation* of the wrists or *fading* and *drawing,* but a lot of concepts and techniques featured in videos aren't much help to the average golfer. Try to find a tip or two that you can remember and practice. Video rental stores stock various golf titles. Beware: some videos contradict each other, just as some books and instructors do. You have to determine which is pertinent to you.

In 1931, Bobby Jones made a series of movie shorts that featured cameos from Hollywood stars. The tapes were discovered in storage, compiled, and transferred to video. *How I Play Golf* gets two emphatic thumbs up. (As you're watching, remember that Jones did not have the benefit of sophisticated editing. He's executing perfect shots one right after the other—live).

Two other videos we can recommend are *The Art of Putting* by Ben Crenshaw, and *Junior Golf The Easy Way* by Mark Steinbauer.

LET'S GO TO 15

When golfers aren't playing or practicing golf, reading a golf book or magazine, watching a golf video, or thinking about golf—and they're not asleep—chances are they're watching golf on television. There are even people who have never picked up a club in their lives who enjoy watching it. Even golfers who usually can't be bothered look forward to the Masters with the anticipation of football fans awaiting the Super Bowl. It's one of golf's majors. The others are the U.S. Open, the British Open, and the PGA Championship.

Despite the perspective that tends to homogenize the golf course, watching a tournament on television will show you more golf, and from better angles, than you would possibly see, even if you were there in person. Under tremendous pressure, the crowd buzzing and hundreds of thousands of dollars hanging in the balance, the golf is routinely impressive, sometimes spectacular.

Entertaining (as perennially high ratings attest), it can be more than a little misleading, especially concerning club selection. Different golfers hit clubs different distances. What might be a wedge for one will be a 7-iron for another and perhaps a 5-iron for someone else. Even among the pros, there is a wide variance. No one asks after a round how far or high you hit it: they ask what your score was. A lot of golfers get caught up with the glamour of a shot rather than simply with getting the ball into the cup in the fewest number of strokes. That is, after all, the object of golf. Of course, when a pro slides an apparent gimme two feet past the hole, we can't resist a "Hey, I coulda made that." If a chronic case of armchair golfer was all it produced, that wouldn't be so bad, but watching the pros can also instill some bad habits.

In a professional tournament, the players are going to take their time, within established limits. Thousands of dollars ride on each shot down the stretch, which obviously is not the case for the rest of us.

When a pro sizes up a putt from three different angles, consults with his or her caddy, then takes another look, just to be certain, it's understandable. Or at least a lot more understandable than it is when we do it. There are also fewer players on the course in any pro event, which colors a viewer's impression. Even in a big field, there will still be fewer golfers on the course than you'd find on your course on an average Sunday. With one notable exception, imitating the pros will serve only to slow down the game.

The exception? Course etiquette, of course. Watch the care players put in each step on and around the green, especially near the hole. Honor is scrupulously observed. Bunkers are carefully raked. Notice how each player acts and where they stand while another plays or putts. When it comes to putting lines, the pros even go one step further. They carefully avoid the area behind the hole in case the putt overshoots it. The player would then have to play his or her *comebacker* through spike marks.

On TV, remember also that you're seeing only the best of the best. The camera has to stay with the tournament story, the leaders, so we rarely see players doing poorly. Their scores may flash by, but as every golfer knows, the score alone doesn't tell the whole story of a round.

SPECTATING

Watching golf live is really not like attending other sporting events. You don't get a seat. The action takes place not just in front of you but all around you, even as far as a half-an-hour walk away. With rare exceptions, team loyalty is nonexistent. There's no "We're number one" chants. No waves. Most people come out just to see good golf, not caring particularly who wins (until something happens to change their minds).

Spectating can be confusing, not to mention exhausting, without a game plan. Realize right off that it is impossible to see everything. Don't even try. Our best advice is to start at the driving range. There you'll be able to get fairly close and observe wonderful—and different—swings that will do things to the ball that will slacken your jaw and quicken your pulse. You can also observe how pros practice, what clubs they hit, what they work on—and then, if you're so inclined, follow them out onto the course to see how their practice translates to their round. Make some mental notes watching the practice green. You might get a glimpse of the eventual winner's hot hand.

Dress comfortably. Grandstands and bleachers ring all greens, but beyond that, you're on your own. A *shooting stick* will make it easier on the legs. A particularly scenic hole provides an idyllic setting to watch the parade of players pass.

Rather than follow one player, savvy spectators pick a spot where a green from one hole adjoins a tee from another. With little effort they can watch one group hit their approach shots and putt, then slip over to the nearby tee in time to marvel at a few tee shots. Some spectators do a little of both—follow a player for a while, then camp out at one hole for a spell. That's part of the pleasure of watching golf. Most tournaments are four rounds, Thursday through Sunday. You'll have an easier time getting around earlier in the week than on the weekends when the larger crowds turn out.

Cameras are not allowed on the course during actual tournament play. To take advantage of photo opportunities, it's safe to carry a camera only on Monday, Tuesday, or Wednesday, when you'll find the players more accommodating.

WATCHING A GENTLEMAN'S GAME

A course map will help you pick your spots. It also provides the day's pairings and starting times. At the Masters, spectators are given a course map that includes a note from Bobby Jones. It reads:

In golf, customs of etiquette and decorum are just as important as rules governing play. It is appropriate for spectators to applaud successful strokes in proportion to difficulty but excessive demonstrations by a player or his partisans are not proper because of the possible effect upon other competitors.

Most distressing to those who love the game of golf is the applauding or cheering of misplays or misfortunes of a player. Such occurrences have been rare at the Masters but we must eliminate them entirely if our patrons are to continue to merit their reputation as the most knowledgeable and considerate in the world.

SUGGESTIONS

No matter how well you may know a player, do not accost him on the golf course. Give him a chance to concentrate on his game. Walk—never run. Be silent and motionless when a contestant prepares to execute a stroke. Be considerate of other spectators. Golf is a gentleman's game.

AUTOGRAPHS

A couple of rules of thumb: Don't ask for an autograph as a player comes off the 18th green, especially after a bad round. When they've finished in the scoring tent and have had a drink and a chance to relax, many players return to the practice area. A good time to ask for autographs is after they've finished practicing for the day. Another is during the Pro–Am after a pro has teed off and is waiting for the amateurs to play.

The worst time and place to ask for an autograph (except perhaps during dinner, when it is simply inexcusable) is during the actual tournament. When the players have completed a hole and are passing through the crowd to get to the next tee, give them a wide berth. Remember, the clock is running. They're penalized for slow play and are concentrating hard on their games. Let them pass without distractions. If you call or write the PGA or the LPGA, they will send you a list of addresses where you can write to players.

LPGA
2570 Volusia Ave., Suite B
Daytona Beach, FL 32114
(904)254-8800

PGA Tour at Sawgrass
112 T.P.C. Boulevard
Ponte Vedra Beach, FL 32082
(904)285-3700

SHOOT-OUTS

Many pro events hold a shoot-out for a handful of top players as part of the week's festivities. It takes place on either the Monday or Tuesday before the tournament. The public is invited.

Shoot-outs are a chance for the players to let their hair down a little, although the competitive juices are still flowing and the prize money is nothing to sneeze at. After each hole, the player with the highest score is eliminated. Ties are decided by short-game play-offs, either long putts or chips closest to the hole. The short games are at least as impressive and entertaining as the spirited (but good-natured) gamesmanship. It's a lot of fun for players and spectators alike.

ANY VOLUNTEERS?

The pro tours could not exist without the cooperation of club members and other volunteers who help the show go on. Volunteering is a great way to get involved behind the scenes. There are perks: free tickets, refreshments, and opportunities to get close to the players, maybe even a free round on the course or a thank-you picnic. If the truth were told, there really isn't a whole lot of work to be done once tournament time arrives, but it is a lot of fun and a nice way to meet other golfers. That doesn't mean staging a pro event doesn't take a monumental effort. It took 2,500 volunteers up to five years to prepare for a recent U.S. Open.

Before we leave the tournament circuit, you should know that even when the pros fold up their tents and move on, opportunities to see good golf are still available locally, wherever you live. College teams, city championships, USGA amateur events, and qualifiers are great ways to see good golf up close or to really feel part of the team as a volunteer.

CHEERIO

During the Battle of Britain, while the Royal Air Force dueled with the Luftwaffe, RAF pilot officer Kenneth Lee was shot down over Kent, England. He was taken to a local golf club "in shirtsleeves slightly bloodstained, but couldn't help hearing members at the last hole complaining that the distraction in the battle of the air was disturbing their putting. . . . once inside a voice demanded, 'Who's that scruffy looking chap at the bar? I don't think he's a member.' "

Those club members who found that the Battle of Britain upset their putting have undoubtedly passed into the pages of P. G. Wodehouse stories. But there will always be an England. If you are fortunate enough to play golf there, or in its rightful (but occasionally disputed) homeland farther north, you will need to be aware of several considerations. One recent observer noted that when it comes to golf attire, "Englishmen on the golf course look as if they're going to lunch, except they have their jackets off."

To play in Great Britain (we didn't mean to neglect Ireland, which has breathtaking scenery and wonderful golf), courtesy insists that you write ahead to the courses you hope to play. Six months ahead is advisable. The more famous courses are becoming so crowded, let's just say the sooner the better and leave it at that. On a package tour, arrangements will be made for you.

You should not pop in unannounced, clubs in hand. Before you leave, sit down with your itinerary and address a letter to the club secretary (or if you belong to a country club or association, ask your pro or secretary to write it for you). Note your approximate timetable, probable arrival time in the area, and preference for an early, late morning, or afternoon tee time. It would be "cheeky" to be any more specific, demanding a 2 P.M. tee time on the 25th, for example. Also, make sure to mention your handicap and how many players will be with you, if any. The club will probably do its best to accommodate you. Don't worry about not having a full foursome. They'll try to find you a game if you're alone.

Of course, golf is played enthusiastically beyond the British Isles. To give you an idea just how far a slice can take you, if you ever have business in Reykjavík or Cairo, for example, you might pack your clubs (along with a parka and some sun block) and check in with the proper authorities.

The Egyptian Golf Federation
Gezira Sporting Club
Gezira, Cairo, Egypt

Golfsamband Islands
(Golf Union of Iceland)
P.O. Box 1076
IS-101 Reykjavík, Iceland

Wherever you play abroad, expect to walk the course. Pull carts or caddies will be available, but riding carts are an American phenomenon.

Travel agents or ads in the back of golf magazines will give you ample ideas for golf travel. Package tours of varying durations suit every budget and taste. If British weather doesn't appeal to you, there's always a golf cruise to the Caribbean or a weekend in South Carolina or Arizona.

GOING TO SCHOOL

In the back of those very same magazines offering Get-Away Weekends to Myrtle Beach and Scottsdale are advertisements for golf schools. At the risk of a pun, let's say up front that there are several schools of thought about them.

The advantages first. Most schools offer flexible rates and timetables, with midweek and weekend sessions available to fit most budgets and schedules. Most offer a low student-to-teacher ratio. They may also feature famous teachers or a famous teaching method covering all aspects of the mechanics of golf and strategy. Schools are a great way to spend a vacation and meet other golfers.

Now the disadvantages. Be prepared to hit golf balls. You may hit more in a morning than you've hit in your entire life. You might check on what other activities are available. For a lot of people, a full day of golf is too much. The low student ratio can also have its drawbacks. For some, especially beginners, a bigger group is more comfortable, sidestepping the self-conscious feelings that surface from continually being under the careful eye of a pro. Some students also come home with a broader understanding of the swing but confused about how it all relates to them.

There is also a danger of thinking that just because you've spent a lot of time and money going to golf school that the instruction at the school is better than it is at home. Cost, too, should certainly be a consideration. For the price of a golf get-away (including food, lodging and travel), you could probably buy a series of private lessons at a local course or club that might be a better deal.

Beware: the schools do assume a certain amount of knowledge on your part. The absolute beginner will probably find the whole scene overwhelming, unless the program is specifically adapted to beginners. There is a story about a golf school instructor who asked her students to bring sand wedges to the next class. One student, still wet behind the ears, asked, "Is ham and cheese okay?"

Golf schools are prejudiced about what they teach. Their methods may not jibe with your own instruction experience— or with teaching methods used at other schools, which can make golf more complicated.

Your game will improve if you devote a solid chunk of time and effort to it. Whether you can get more bang for your buck at home or whether combining golf with a vacation is too appealing to pass up are obviously things you'll have to determine. All package deals are not created equal. Make sure you know what is and what is not included.

GOLF'S GRASS ROOTS

If your travels ever take you to Gloucester, England, you might wander by the great east window of Gloucester Cathedral. The stained glass dates from the mid-fourteenth century and certainly appears to depict golf, which provides interesting evidence that golf was played in England that long ago.

Steering clear of the hornets' nest of debate, national pride, theory, innuendo, and fancy guesswork that surrounds golf's origins, there are many places where you can go to see relics of the game and judge for yourself. Several museums, both here and abroad, house splendid collections devoted to golf history, artwork, and craftsmanship. The James River Country Club, Golf Museum and Library, near Newport News, Virginia, has a collection of early clubs that is unsurpassed. It's interesting to note that when Harry Vardon, the great British professional, won the 1900 U.S. Open, he used only seven clubs: two woods, four irons, and a putter. They're part of the collection, along with his bag.

Other (and by no means all) museums:

The American Golf Hall of Fame
Foxburg, PA 16036
(412)659-3196

Joe Baucom Golf Museum
"The Legends"
Highway 501
Myrtle Beach, SC 29588

The James River Country Club
  Golf Museum and Library
1500 Country Club Rd.
Newport News, VA 23606
(804)595-3327

Ralph W. Miller Golf Library/Museum
Industry Hills Recreation and Conference Center
1 Industry Hills Pkwy.
City of Industry, CA 91744
(818)965-0861

The PGA Tour at Sawgrass
112 T.P.C Blvd.
Ponte Vedra Beach, FL 32082
(904)285-3700

The PGA/World Golf Hall of Fame
PGA Blvd.
Pinehurst, NC 28374
(800)334-0178

Jude E. Poynter Golf Museum
College of the Desert
43-500 Monterrey Ave.
Palm Desert, CA 92260
(619)341-2491

The Ouimet Museum and Golf House
190 Park Rd.
Weston, MA 02195
(617)891-6400

USGA Golf House
Liberty Corner Rd.
Far Hills, NJ 07931
(908)234-2300

SPECULATING

Golf collectibles are hot. A wisp of the fever that turned baseball
cards into investments has brought old clubs out of the closet
(and attic and garage) and into auction catalogs, sometimes going
for record sums.

The Golf Collectors Society is an organization of zealots who
enjoy delving into and sharing the history of the game without
an eye on making a buck. Before you buy or sell, you are urged
to contact the GCS. They can put you in touch with members
in your area who might be able to assist you. The GCS bulletin
is must reading for those interested in pursuing collecting, an
avocation that will end only when the wallet and other vital
organs give way to reality. Many GCS members have items for
sale at reasonable prices, much less than you will find anywhere
aside from Salvation Army stores or church sales (frequented by
all savvy collectors).

Be warned: millions of wood-shafted clubs were manufactured; not every one you find will ensure your retirement.

Don't let that deter you from enjoying a club that is not worth six figures; it's just to dissuade you from parting with more of your money than might be necessary.

Golf Collectors Society
P.O. Box 491
Shawnee Mission, KS 66201
(913)649-4618

GOING, GOING, GONE

Golf has attracted the attention of auction houses, big and small. Their lavish catalogs make informative reading, and if you follow up and request the "prices-realized list," you will have an idea of what one sector of the golf collectible market will bear. Auctions, however, are not an accurate barometer of value. While helpful, the catalogs are not free; they may, however, be cheaper after the auction has been held.

Several price guides are on the market. Note: the danger with these books is that values fluctuate. Many price guides thus have an expiration date only slightly longer than a carton of milk. Check the publication date to ensure freshness and keep an eye out for new, updated editions.

Antique Golf Club Price Guide, Peter Georgiady, Castalio Press.
The Encyclopedia of Golf Collectibles, John M. and Morton W. Olman, Books Americana, Inc.

A beautiful magazine, *Golfiana,* the International Journal for Golf Historians and Collectors, comes out quarterly. Every issue includes wonderfully reproduced golf art and exceptional articles on the history of the game.

Golfiana
P.O. Box 668
Edwardsville, IL 62025
(618)656-8172

Golf Journal, the Official Publication of the United States Golf Association, is available to associate members of the USGA. It is another pleasant way of keeping up with the game, past and present, while contributing to its future. The Golf School quiz each month is a trivia buff's dream, the golf equivalent of the Sunday crossword. *Golf Journal* is also refreshingly bereft of advertisements and instruction tips.

Golf Journal
P.O. Box 708
Far Hills, NJ 07931-0708
(908)234-2300

MEMBERS ONLY

There are associations for left-handed golfers, hole-in-one makers, even a group for golfers seeking companionship of a more personal and perhaps, if you're willing to concede a putt now and then, permanent nature. The National Hole-In-One Association will commemorate your historic shot in the archives of the PGA World Golf Hall of Fame.

National Hole-In-One Association
8350 N. Central Expressway
Suite 730
Dallas, TX 75206
(800)HIO-GOLF

Others

Golf Nut Society of America
P.O. Box 1226
Carefree, AZ 85377
(602)488-0401

National Amputee Golf Association
P.O. Box 1228
Amherst, NH 03031
(603)673-1135

National Association of Left-Handed Golfers
P.O. Box 801223
Houston, TX 77280
(713)464-8683

National Senior Sports Association
1248 Post Road
Fairfield, CT 06403
(800)282-NSSA

Sports Lovers Exchange
(unattached single golfers)
P.O. Box 933
Southampton, NY 11968

Several organizations seek to share golf with those who otherwise might not have the opportunity. Professional golf has always had a close relationship with charities, a tradition that continues stronger than ever today. In many states, local charities offer golf-related bargains to raise money. Nationally, the Calvin Peete National Minority Golf Foundation, named for the successful professional, serves as a vehicle for underprivileged children to acquire and build upon skills and values otherwise not available in their homes. Another program, Hook a Kid on Golf, is run through the auspices of the National Youth Sports Coaches Association.

The Calvin Peete National Minority Golf Foundation
1550 Terrell Mill Rd. #128
Marietta, GA 30067
(404)850-9110

Chi Chi Rodriguez Youth Foundation, Inc.
3030 McMullen-Booth Rd.
Clearwater, FL 34621
(813)726-8829

National Youth Sports Coaches Association
2611 Old Okeechobee Rd.
West Palm Beach, FL 33409
(407)684-1141

A FINAL THOUGHT

Several years ago, for an as-yet unpublished article, a handful of touring professionals were asked: "What was the best advice you ever received in golf?" Some mentioned technical adjustments in their swings. Others cited psychological aids that helped push them to the top of their profession. Chi Chi Rodriguez had an entirely different response, one we think bears repeating. "The best advice I ever got in golf," he sent back, "was that golf is a gentleman's game, and you always play it in an honorable way."

We hope you agree.

If you have questions about etiquette or anecdotes about lapses of etiquette that you'd like to see discussed in future editions of this book, please write:

Barbara Puett & Jim Apfelbaum
3509 Fawn Creek Path
Austin, TX 78746

CHAPTER NINE CHECKLIST

__ Remember to stop and smell the flowers—books, museums, associations, etc.

__ To play abroad, write at least six months in advance; include handicap and approximate timetable.

__ The USGA can help you with names and addresses.

__ If you plan to play abroad, expect to walk.

__ Golf videos often feature concepts and techniques too advanced for the average golfer.

__ Weigh the pros and cons of golf schools before making a commitment.

__ "The bottom line on golf etiquette is that, with it, you can play with anyone, anywhere in the world."

CHAPTER NINE GLOSSARY

Comebacker—Putt that remains after a ball has skirted or run past the hole.

Drawing—Deliberate attempt to play a shot that turns gradually from right to left in flight. Not to be confused with a hook.

Fading—Deliberate attempt to play a shot that turns gradually from left to right in flight. Not to be confused with a slice.

Pronation—Rotating of the hand and forearm through the swing.

Shooting Stick—Walking stick with collapsible seat on top.

INDEX

ABOUT THE AUTHORS

BARBARA PUETT is a golf instructor to 500–1000 beginning students each year. A graduate of the University of Texas at Austin and a former physical education and science teacher in the Austin public school system, she has competed and won amateur golf tournaments at the state and local level for two decades. She was named Golf Teacher of the Year by the Austin American-Statesman in 1989. Her comments on golf etiquette have been featured in *USA Today* and *Golf Illustrated*. The mother of three children, she lives in Austin with her husband, Roane.

JIM APFELBAUM is a freelance writer, editor, and entrepreneur. A Philadelphia native, Jim now lives in Austin with his wife, Sandra, three cats, and a growing collection of golf memorabilia. He prefers to walk and carry his own clubs. A contributor to *Golf Illustrated* and *Golf Journal,* this is his first book.